the *Great* BARBECUE COMPANION

Mops, Sops, Sauces, and Rubs

By Bruce Bjorkman

THE CROSSING PRESS
Berkeley | Toronto

The Crossing Press
A division of Ten Speed Press
P.O. Box 7123
Berkeley, California 94707
www.tenspeed.com

Distributed in Australia by Simon and Schuster Australia, in Canada by Ten Speed Press Canada, in New Zealand by Southern Publishers Group, in South Africa by Real Books, and in the United Kingdom and Europe by Airlift Book Company.

Library of Congress Cataloging-in-Publication Data
Bjorkman, Bruce
        The great barbecue companion: mops, sops, sauces,
and rubs / Bruce Bjorkman.
            p. cm.
        Includes index.
        ISBN 0-89594-806-0 (pbk.)
        1. Barbecue cookery. 2. Barbecue sauce 3. Marinades. I. Title.
        TX840.B3B555   1996
        641.7'6—dc20   95-47839
                                                            CIP

Cover and interior design by Victoria May
Photos by Bruce Bjorkman, Sandra Bjorkman,
    Dennis Hayes, and John Schmitz

Printed in the U.S.A.

5 6 7 8 9 10—09 08 07 06 05 04

Acknowledgments

The adage "many hands make light work" is a very true reality in the production and accomplishment of this book. I'd very much like to thank the following people for helping me with this, my first book: Dennis Hayes, for the initial idea and support, and for his help in gathering the recipes. Thanks also to Ms. Elaine Goldman-Gill for giving a "macho man" the chance to actually pen his first volume—a dream come true. Very special thanks to Julie Larson Bricher of *Oregon Food Journal,* for her help in formulating the manuscript and her constant encouragement. Thanks also to my editor, Marianne Rogoff, for her skilled help in polishing the manuscript.

A big barbecue "thank you!" goes to the following people: My employers at Buckmaster Gourmet Coffee Company, for allowing me the time off needed to write this book; Jan Roberts-Dominquez, for her most valuable advice and help on mustard; Ann Wilder of Vann's Spices, for her excellent spice information; to my many barbecue buddies from across the country, for their help and recipe contributions; and especially to Kim Wallis for the rubs in the chapter, Rubs and Pastes.

Most importantly, I wish to thank the love of my life, my "Bar-B-Cutie," Sandi, for her love and patience, and for giving up an entire summer's worth of weekends for this book. It is dedicated to her.

Contents

Introduction **7**

Sauce and Barbecue Basics **15**

Sweet Sauces **25**

Savory Sauces **39**

Flame-thrower Sauces **59**

Secret Recipes of the Pitmasters **71**

Rubs and Pastes **83**

Resources **103**

Bibliography **108**

Calendar of Barbecue Competitions
sanctioned by the Kansas City Barbecue Society **109**

Recipes in Order of Appearance

Sweet Sauces

Apricot Sweet 'n' Sour Sauce 27
Apricot-Pineapple Sauce 27
Guava Barbecue Sauce 28
Last Mango in Paris Barbecue Sauce 28
Orange-Tangy Barbecue Sauce 29
Key West Barbecue Sauce 29
Georgia Peach Sauce 30
Pineapple Marinade 30
Plum Ginger Barbecue Sauce 31
Homemade Plum Sauce 31
Florida Sunshine Sauce 32
Mandarin Orange Sauce 32
Raspberry Basting Sauce 33
Tangerine-Tamarind Sauce 33
Pacific Rim Barbecue Sauce 34
Firehouse Barbecue Sauce 34
Santa Fe Chile Barbecue Sauce 35
Deep South Cola Barbecue Sauce 36
Lola's Cola Sauce 36
Naw'lins Barbecue Sauce 37
Whisky Town BBQ Sauce 37
A Taste of Vermont Sopping Syrup 38
Hard Stuff Barbecue Sauce 38

Savory Sauces

Carolina Spicy Vinegar Marinade 41
Eastern North Carolina-style Sauce 41
Eastern Carolina Hot Vinegar
  Barbecue Sauce 42
Piedmont-Lexington-style Sauce 42
Texas-style BBQ Sauce 43
Rib Stickin' Sauce 44
Chipotle Molasses Glaze 44

Barbecue Sauce 45
Mel's Moppin' Sauce 45
Chuckwagon BBQ Sauce 45
Guasacaca (Venezuela-style Barbecue Sauce) 46
Creole Barbecue Sauce 46
All-American Sauce 47
Sweet 'n' Savory Sauce 47
Flamin' Groovy Basting Sauce 47
All-American Mustard Sauce 48
Mushroom BBQ Sauce 48
Subtly Citrus Barbecue Sauce 49
Damn Tasty, Sure Simple Rib Sauce 49
Savory Herb Barbecue Sauce 50
Icuddahadda Sauce 51
Fourth of July BBQ Sauce 51
Sesame and Ginger Marinade 52
Tandoori Marinade 52
Lina's Chinese Barbecue Sauce for Pork 53
Thyme-Mustard Sauce 53
Mint-Rosemary Sauce 53
Cattle Drive Barbecue Sauce 54
State Fair Barbecue Sauce 54
Nuts-About-You Barbecue Sauce 55
Loozieanna Cookin' Sauce 56
Jack Daniels Barbecue Glaze 56
Coffee Barbecue Sauce 57
Curried Tomato Sauce 57
Headhunter's Satay 57
Colonel Mustard in the Library Sauce 58
Spicy Peanut Sauce 58

Flamethrower Sauces

Hot Orange-Chile Sauce 61
Elvira-Inspired Barbecue Sauce 61

Wildman Willie's Quein' Sauce	62
Fiery Lime-Cilantro Sauce	63
Kim's Hot Wing Sauce	63
Dakota Kid's Buffalo Breath	
Garlic-Jalapeño Paste	64
Hot Orange Spice Barbecue Sauce	64
Buzzin' Bee Honey-Q-Sauce	65
Miami Spice Seafood Barbecue Sauce	65
Harissa Moroccan Spiced Red Chile Paste	66
Colorado Chile Que Sauce	66
Berberé Arabic Chile and Spice Paste	67
Who Do Voodoo Sauce	68
Dominican Barbecue Sauce	68
Jerk Marinade	69
Mole Verde	70

Championship Sauces from the Pros

Wilber's South Carolina Chicken Sauce	73
Paul Kirk's Grilled Chicken Sauce	73
The Baron's Sweet & Spicy Barbecue Sauce	74
Remus's Kansas City Classic Sauce	75
Diddy-Wa-Diddy Mop and Basting Sauce	75
Dan Green's Sauce for Pork	76
Beaver Castor's All-Purpose Rub	76
Bob Lyon's Cajun Barbecue Sauce	77
Ron's Mandarin-Hickory Chipotle	
Barbecue Sauce	78
The Campbell Family's Texas Sop	78
J. P. Hayes's Chipotle BBQ Sauce	79
Hollis's Cilantro & Lime Barbecue Sauce	80
Bruce's Spicy Raisin Sauce	80
Louisiana Jann's Sweet 'n' Tangy Sauce	81
John Stage's Jalapeena Bar-B-Q Sauce	81
Hollis's Watermelon Barbecue Sauce	82
Bruce's Miss Peach, Mr. Bourbon Sauce	82

Rubs and Pastes

Bruce's BBQ Rub (circa 1993)	85
Sandi's Leg o' Lamb Rub	85
Rub for Beef & Pork	86
Across the Road Rub	86
Mustard Seed Rub	87
Tandoori Spice Rub	87
The Baron's No Salt Rub	88
Dennis Hayes's Basic Barbecue Rub	88
Jamaican Jerk Rub	89
Jamaican Jerk Rub #2	89
Jerk Rub # 3	90
Rosemary Rub	90
Big Easy Rub	91
Purely Pork Rub	91
Rub-a-Dub Barbecue Rub	93
Country Spice Rub	93
Nice 'n' Naughty Rub	94
Sesame and Mustard Rub	94
Li'l Devil Rub	95
Garlic-Anchovy Rub	95
Hot 'n' Honey Rub	95
Cajun Rub	96
New Mexico Chile Rub	96
Latin-style Spice Rub	96
South Texas Rub	97
Basic Texas BBQ Dry Rub	97
Spicy San Antonio Rub	98
Texas Tumbleweed Spice Mix	98
Sambal Mint Paste	99
Traditional Tandoori	99
Green Chile Paste	100
Mixed Peppercorn Rub	100
Molasses Baste	100
Yucatan Achiote Paste	101
Spicy Orange Paste	102

Introduction

*T*he focus of this book is barbecue sauces which, unlike their bottled, preservative-laden cousins, you can make up fresh in your own kitchen whenever the mood hits you.

From the far-flung corners of the world, more than a hundred different types of barbecue sauces, dry rubs, and paste recipes are gathered here for you to add to your barbecue and grilling repertoire. They range from the sweet and savory to the flame-thrower varieties. Some amusing barbecue tidbits are thrown in, which you can use like fine spices to season your dinner-table conversations. Look for the sauce brushes that highlight special saucemaster tips from the experts.

Barbecuing versus Grilling

If I had a dollar each time people used the word barbecue when they were referring to grilling, I could afford to open a string of barbecue joints of my own. My wife Sandi, who grew up in Maine, says that practical New Englanders have a better handle on a word to describe grilling: cookout.

Barbecuing and grilling are antithetical to one another. Barbecuing utilizes a fire at a lower temperature than grilling, often between 180 and 250°F. The fire is kept a distance away from the meat. Various kinds of wood are used, either as the fuel source or added on top of briquets, to impart a rich, smoky flavor. True barbecuing is a much slower, patience-testing process than grilling, which utilizes very high temperatures between 300 and 750°F. Grilling sears the meat and cooks it very quickly, usually without the use of wood smoke to impart additional flavor to the food.

Barbecue Sauces

The primary focus of this book is making great sauces. There is a difference in the time you should apply certain sauces to the meat you are barbecuing. Vinegar- or mustard-based sauces can be applied to the meat before or during the barbecue or grilling process. But the sweet-based sauces should be used only in the final stages of barbecuing or grilling. The reason? The sweet sauces either contain sugar or natural sugar from fruit or tomatoes. If these sweet sauces are applied before or during the barbecuing or grilling process, the sauce will carmelize and burn the outside of the meat.

Marinades

Marinades tend to be acidic in nature. The meat is soaked in a marinade before barbecuing. The acid in the marinade breaks down the fiber in the meat. Meat is porous, and when it's left in a marinade overnight it will absorb more spices and seasonings than if you simply sauced the meat after cooking. Jim Tarantino, author of *Marinades* (The Crossing Press), suggests that in order to replace moisture lost in the marinating process, vegetable oil should be added to most liquid marinades. I highly recommend Jim's book for further study; it is one of the best ever written on marinades.

Overleaf: The Interstate Bar-B-Q in Memphis Tennessee

Sops

Like marinades, sops also are acidic in nature. Most sops are composed primarily of vinegar or Worcestershire sauce. Sops are applied to the meat with a long wooden-handled mop while it is being barbecued or grilled. In many parts of Texas and the Southwest, kitchen or restaurant tables will have a bottle of sop handy for additional dousing.

Rubs

Rubs are composed of dry ingredients—herbs, spices, and other seasonings. The term is a misnomer, since rubs should be sprinkled on rather than rubbed into meat prior to cooking. You may use rubs to provide a higher degree of concentrated flavor to larger cuts of meat like pork shoulder, whole beef brisket, and beef or pork spareribs. These large cuts of meat can taste pretty bland without the benefit of seasoning prior to cooking, and a rub is an easy way to accomplish this.

You can use a rub and then follow with a sauce in the final phase of cooking or at the table. Strive for balance when you use a rub and a sauce or sop on a piece of meat. Your tongue should easily discern the flavors of the meat, smoke, and seasonings equally.

World-Class Barbecue Ingesters

It's interesting to note that three pairs of authors qualify as having eaten a lifetime's worth of barbecue in a very short amount of time. *Roadfood/Goodfood* writers Jane and Michael Stern cruise the nation's backroads looking for out-of-the-way eateries. Their journeys have led them to hundreds of barbecue spots. Authors Vince Staten and Greg Johnson of *Real Barbecue* fame claim to have eaten at more than 700 barbecue restaurants, ingesting a belly-bursting 629,200 calories apiece! Not to be outdone, South Carolinians Allie Patricia Wall and Ron Layne, authors of *Hog Heaven,* traveled throughout their home state, gorging on the best barbecue from more than 100 South Carolina joints. You know what they say, "It's a greasy job, but somebody's got to do it."

Warning: Do not reuse any excess rub after it has been applied to the meat. You risk food contamination poisoning. Similarly, after you've marinated meats or poultry, don't use the marinade as a table sauce. It may be contaminated by bacteria.

American Barbecue Sauce Bases

Three primary, distinctive bases are used for American barbecue sauces: tomatoes, mustard, and vinegar.

Tomato-based Barbecue Sauces

Tomatoes are king in many barbecue sauces; they are the primary ingredient in the most popular national brands of barbecue sauce in the nation today.

Folktales abound about the import and cultivation of tomatoes in America. Many of the tales, embellished over the years, are still hotly debated by historians and botanists.

It is believed that tomato seeds were first transported to Europe by the Spaniards, who were introduced to the plant by the Aztecs. Our third U.S. President, Thomas Jefferson, is credited as being responsible for importing tomato seeds into the country shortly before the Revolutionary War. According to Andrew Smith in *The Tomato in America*, tomatoes were used in America's kitchens by the 1830s. During this time, tomato-mania took hold, with physicians producing "tomato pills," touting them as miracle cures for whatever ailed you.

Tomatoes weren't always so popular. It wasn't until a prominent citizen of Salem, New Jersey, Robert Gibbon Johnson, stood on the steps of the county courthouse in 1802 and devoured a tomato in front of hundreds of witnesses that the tomato was considered edible. It was a shocking act at the time, since tomatoes, which belong to the deadly nightshade plant family, were considered poisonous. Smith states that there is no reliable historic documentation to confirm such an occurrence. Even though the plausibility of the event is now questioned, the residents of Salem, New Jersey still hold "Robert Gibbons Johnson Day" each year, complete with a reenactment of the incident.

In *Low Country Cooking*, author John Martin Taylor states that as early as 1764, in Charleston, South Carolina, gardener Henry Laurens grew tomatoes for eating. Even so, it wouldn't be until the late 1800s to early 1900s that tomatoes were grown commercially in the U.S. for consumption.

By the year 1822, tomato recipes were appearing in community newspapers by the thousands. Farming publications also began to tout the once-lowly tomato as a cure for hog scours. Smith documents an incident wherein the tomato became the subject of a Supreme Court case. The Justices ruled in 1892 on whether the bright red orb was a fruit or a vegetable. In the case Nix v. Hedden, the plaintiff's counsel argued that tomatoes were indeed a fruit and therefore not subject to the Tariff Act of 1883. The Justices thought otherwise, and in their decision stated that "tomatoes are the fruit of a vine, just as are cucumbers . . . but in the common language of the people . . . all these are vegetables . . . usually served at dinner . . . and not like fruits generally, as desserts."

At last estimate, each American will consume more than eighteen pounds of fresh tomatoes and seventy pounds of processed tomatoes this year. The United States grows the largest supply of tomatoes in the world today.

It is believed that the advent of commercial barbecue sauces began back in the 1950s, when the J. L. Kraft Company, a manufacturer of vegetable cooking oils, began to affix bags of spices to bottles of their oil sold in grocery stores. The spices were used to flavor the oil. By the mid 1950s, Kraft introduced the first mass-marketed, tomato-based barbecue sauce sold nationwide. Today the company is still the largest seller of barbecue sauces in America.

Mustard-based Barbecue Sauces

The word *mustard* is derived from the Latin term *mustin ardens*, meaning "burning must." "Must" was made from freshly pressed, unfermented grape juice, into which ground mustard seeds were mixed, forming a spreadable paste. Mustard was used as both a seasoning and medicinal agent in many ancient societies. Pliny offered some forty different mustard recipes in the first century A.D. Mustard has been a staple in Chinese cuisine dating back to prehistoric times. In the seventeenth century, France began producing mustard in such mass quantities that it became known as the mustard-producing capital of the world, manufacturing and exporting huge quantities of table and cooking mustards. Food historian Jan Roberts Dominquez notes in *The Mustard Book* that by 1812 France was bottling at least ninety-three varieties of mustard.

In the United States, however, the flavor of imported mustards was considered too vigorous for the American palate. It wasn't until the early 1900s, when New Jersey resident Francis French instructed his plant foreman to develop a paler, milder form of processed mustard, that the spicy condiment took its rightful place in American cuisine. Within two years after the reformulated condiment hit store shelves, French's was selling millions of dollars worth of the product.

Vinegar-based Barbecue Sauces

Vinegar has been a staple since ancient Egyptian times. It is most likely that the use of vinegar in American cooking began with the Puritans. Vinegar's acidic composition helps to break down tough meat fibers. It also acts as a preservative. Many food historians believe that vinegar-based sauces were used primarily to disguise spoiled meat and fish. White vinegar, the most common type, is derived from processing wine at least twice. Many knowledgeable cooks reject this type of vinegar in favor of cider, red wine, or balsamic types.

A Bit of Advice

Pacific Northwest-based barbecuer Judie Anderson of the Good Cheap Fun cooking team says there are two things every serious barbecuer needs to do in order to produce quality que: "Don't use frozen meat—ever—and cook it low and slow." Anderson ought to know: she captured first place in the Pork Ribs category two years in a row at the Jack Daniels Invitational, held each October in Lynchburg, Tennessee.

Regional American Barbecue Sauces

America has always been a great melting pot, and the mixed cultures of early immigrants has produced a variety of "American-style" barbecues. Whether on the dusty, gritty plains of Texas, or in the pine-scented woods of the Carolinas, you'll find any number of barbecue-sauce meccas. Lexington, Memphis, Taylor . . . the names reel off the tongue like a Barbecue *Who's Who*. There is, to be sure, intense rivalry among these citadels of barbecue, each one proclaiming superiority in the realm of smoke, meat, and sauce. Is there such a thing as the quintessential American sauce-producing region? The prudent barbecue lover will simply smile and enjoy the grand bragging, because each barbecue capitol has its own inimitable flavor which should be enjoyed on its own merits.

A representative sample of regional sauces appears later in the book; a few regions are so well known for their barbecue sauces that they deserve a little limelight here.

Texas

There is truth to the adage that the Lone Star State does things in a big way. Not only is Texas the second-largest state in the country—it also boasts the largest number of barbecue establishments in the nation, 1300 at last count. Texas cuisine has been influenced greatly by its neighbor to the south, Mexico, and by the pioneering German immigrants who firmly established themselves in the state's hill country. As far as sauce is concerned, a wise old Texan once summed it up by saying, "There are those that are sugar- and tomato-based, and those that aren't."

In the hill country of Central Texas, in cities like Abilene and Brownwood, you'll find aromatic, thin, hot pepper-based sauces with paprika added to produce a deep red color. In East-central Texas, near Taylor (home to an annual barbecue cook-off that's one of the best attended in the country), barbecue sauces are dark and spicy, comprised of onions, chiles, and the dense flavor of cumin, which is also used to season homemade link sausages. More often, however, Texans use simple seasonings, such as black pepper and salt, or a mop made from equal parts of vegetable oil and vinegar.

North Carolina

North Carolina has four distinctive regions. Starting from the Western ridge of the Appalachians near Ashville, barbecue sauces are primarily tomato ketchup-based. As you progress eastward across the state toward the central region around Charlotte, sauces are thinner and milder, composed primarily of tomatoes, ketchup, and vinegar. As you travel east of Raleigh, the barbecue lover will find thin, vinegar-based sauces spiked with red and black pepper. Down around Kinston and Wilmington, sauces are almost devoid of tomatoes. Here, a mixture of Texas Pete brand hot pepper sauce, Worcestershire sauce, and apple cider vinegar are commonly used.

South Carolina

Like its northern neighbor, South Carolina is home to almost 100 commercial barbecue establishments and boasts six specific, regional styles of barbecue sauce.

Kentucky

There aren't so many varieties of sauces in Kentucky. In the commercial barbecue pits across the state, mutton is generally the meat of choice, most often cooked over hickory coals and then sprinkled with a jaunty red pepper and vinegar-based sauce. Some establishments, like the postage-stamp-size Starne's Barbecue in Paducah, sprinkle the finished mutton with an almost-hot red pepper sauce. Many barbecue joints like Starne's use a vinegar-pepper-tomato concoction for their sauces.

Tennessee

The Volunteer State is not only famous for its country music and the blues; its largest city, Memphis, is a major barbecue paradise. Don't just take anyone's word for it. Check out the Memphis telephone book, which lists eighty restaurants that place "Que" at the top of their menus.

Memphis is also the Pork Capitol of the South, home to the all-pork Memphis In May World Championship Barbecue Contest. Legendary barbecue joints abound, such as Leonard's, Gridley's, Charlie Vergo's, and The Interstate Barbecue. Memphis-style barbecue is either "wet" or "dry." Wet means meat dripping with a sweet, tangy, tomato-based sauce. Dry refers to a mixture of spices and herbs, known as a dry rub, which is put on the meat before (or in the case of Vergo's, after) it hits the pits.

Missouri

Famous for its country music, Missouri is considered the melting pot of all barbecue styles. Beef, pork, and lamb are smoke-cooked to perfection in Kansas City. The world-famous Kansas City Barbecue Society (KCBS) is located here. The Kansas City-based organization is so serious about barbecue that its motto is, "Barbecue, It's Not Just for Breakfast Anymore." Within Kansas City's boundaries, you will find no fewer than 46 barbecue joints, including the legendary Arthur Bryant's, Gates & Sons, and Rosedale.

You will find a large number of sauce variations in Kansas City, including Karen Putnum's locally produced, award-winning, raspberry-infused "Flower of the Flame" sauce, as well as Dr. Rich Davis's renowned K.C. Masterpiece sauces. Kansas City's most revered saucemeister is Arthur Bryant, who on the day after his death, was honored with a cartoon tribute in the *Kansas City Times*. The drawing showed Saint Peter escorting K.C.'s venerable barbecue saint through the Pearly Gates, asking, "Did you bring sauce?"

Kansas City hosts the country's largest sauce competition, Diddy-Wa-Diddy, held annually on the first weekend in October as part of the American Royal Invitational Barbecue Cookoff. Remus Powers, the originator and official saucemeister of the Diddy-Wa-Diddy, began holding the contest on his patio in 1984. It is the only commercial barbecue sauce contest of its kind in the world, attracting more than 400 commercial sauce entries in twenty-three categories, including such unusual classifications as Hot Fish, Hot Wine, Hot Fruit, and Hot Vinegar sauces. Remus says that with so many barbecue restaurants in the city, "Any recipe which represents itself as classic Kansas City is at best a compromise. There are a few constants, such as vinegar, tomato, and paprika and some sweetness. The rest is pure inspiration."

Exotic Barbecue Sauces

Of course, barbecue sauces are not unique to America. In particular, Indonesia, Jamaica, and Thailand also offer a wide variety of unique sauces to flavor meats cooked over wood or charcoal fires. These are making their way into the American barbecue-lover's consciousness.

Jamaican Jerk

African slaves were brought to the West Indies by the British in the 1600s. The slaves carried their peppers and jerk barbecue with them. The heart and soul of jerk cooking lie in the use of the hottest pepper grown on earth, the scotch bonnet, said to be thirty to fifty times hotter than the jalapeño! Jerk seasoning can be a liquid, paste, or dry mixture, applied to pork, chicken, or beef the night before the meat is cooked over a palmetto (allspice tree) wood fire. Helen Willinsky, author of *Jerk, Barbecue From Jamaica* (The Crossing Press), states that the best place in Jamaica to find authentic jerk barbecue is in the Boston Beach region. You'll find both dry and wet jerk recipes in this book.

Indonesian Satay

Along city streets and in country villages throughout the Spice Islands, Indonesian satay (skewered beef, pork, or goat) is cooked over a charcoal fire. The "official" barbecue sauce of Indonesia typically is a hot, spicy peanut sauce, which complements the cooked meat with a nutty zestiness.

Thai Sauces

Thailand is home to a variety of spicy sauces that enhance the dishes cooked in people's homes and along busy city streets. Typically, Thais use curry and indigenous peppers such as the bird's-eye extensively in their cooking, as well as satay-type sauces similar to those used throughout Indonesia.

Barbecue is serious business in the South. In many respects, barbecue is taken as seriously as religion.

—Stephen A. Smith, "The Rhetoric of Barbecue," *Studies in Popular Culture*

Sauce and Barbecue Basics

*M*ost people already own many of the appliances and tools needed to barbecue. If you don't have a particular item, most are inexpensive and available in any well-stocked kitchen goods department. When you buy quality tools hurts only once. You are better off purchasing a high-quality item, rather than having to replace the same item over and over again.

A Real Horatio Alger Barbecuer

Before the invention of the Weber-Stephen kettle barbecue, most grills were of the brazier type, open and exposed to Mother Nature, often producing disheartening results. Enter George Stephen who, in 1952 while working for the Weber Brothers Metal Works, began experimenting with covered grills. Putting two spun-metal pieces together, Stephen came up with the kettle grill. Dubbed "Sputnik" by doubting neighbors, 43 years later the Weber Kettle grill is easily one of the most recognized and purchased grills in the world.

Basic Barbecue Units

Kettle Grills

Invented by Dr. George Stephen in the 1950s, the kettle grill is now ubiquitous in America's backyards. The most common-size kettle grills are eighteen or twenty-two inches in diameter. Most kettle barbecues are priced from fifty dollars up.

Watersmokers

Looking like cousins of Star Wars' R2D2, watersmokers are very versatile units, because you can smoke, grill, and roast meat with them. One of the distinctive differences is the use of a waterpan, which adds moisture to the cooking environment. The waterpan is located approximately halfway up the length of the cylindrical tube that holds the two grids. The charcoal briquet pan is located at the bottom of the cylinder. A side door on the cylinder allows you to replace both water and briquets during the long cooking process. Most brands of watersmokers can be purchased for less than thirty dollars.

Barrel Barbecues

There are two types of barrel barbecues, those with and without offset fireboxes. Barrel barbecues, most common in Texas, Oklahoma, and parts of the Deep South, usually are made from a fifty-five-gallon steel drum. However, an increasing number of barrel barbecue makers are opting for high-gauge metal or stainless steel. If you're a novice barbecuer, you might want to start with a kettle grill or watersmoker, and step up to a barrel-type barbecue unit later.

Overleaf: Remus Powers, Ph.B., aka Ardie A. Davis; Lil' Jakes Old Southern Pit Barbecue in Kansas City, Missouri.

Gas Grills

As the name implies, a propane gas unit is used primarily for grilling meats, fish, and chicken at high temperatures. While some manufacturers would have you believe that you can actually barbecue on a gas grill, no serious barbecuer would attempt such a feat. The average price of gas grills, according to a gas trade association, averages around $150.

Electric Grills and Smokers

There are several electric barbecue grills available for indoor or outdoor use. While most of the grills are more suited for higher-heat grilling, the electric smokers can do a nice job of smoking small amounts of meat in a short period of time.

Pellet Barbecues

Pellet grills are relatively new to the barbecue scene. An auger, controlled by a micro-processor, controls both the fan and the rate at which wood pellets are fed into the unit's firebox. Pellets are made from various types of hardwoods.

One drawback to a pellet barbecue is that it must be kept away from moisture, or the pellets will turn to useless sawdust. The price of a pellet barbecue is comparable to a high-end gas grill.

Miscellaneous

In addition to your barbecuing unit, the following accessories and tools will help you: long gloves, a fire extinguisher (ABC-type), thermometers (oven-type for your inside grid temperature), and an instant-read meat thermometer (for assessing interior temperature of meat). Other items: long-handled tongs, brushes, a spray bottle, water pan, and charcoal chimney.

There are two kinds of South Carolina barbecue, good and best.

—Anonymous

Tips for Your Fire

Using Wood for Flavor

Wood smoke is the mystical part of barbecuing. Everyone has their tried-and-true favorite varieties of smoking woods. Personally, I've found that apple and alder woods produce a sweet, neutral smoke that goes well with anything in the pit. Cherry wood is very good, but like maple, pecan, hickory, and mesquite, it has a tendency to turn your meat quite dark in color. Oak is also a popular hardwood used by barbecuers across the country.

Larger pieces of wood should be soaked in water for at least one hour before using. Smaller wood chips can be soaked for ten minutes or more. Basically, you want the wood to be wet so it smolders. It's the smoldering that produces flavorful smoke. Hot water will loosen the fibers in the wood more quickly than cold water. After soaking, place the wood chunks or chips directly onto the briquets. Replenish every sixty to ninety minutes.

Three important notes about using wood: First, most novice barbecuers start smoking their meat far too quickly. Allow the meat to heat up and the fibers to loosen before introducing smoke to the pit. Second, the wood-smoke flavor should complement the meat. You are far better off to undersmoke your meat than smoke it too much; if you do, the meat will taste bitter. Finally, remember the rule of balanced barbecue. Take into consideration your meat, the type of wood, and the sauce or marinade. All these elements should complement each other, not clash.

Lighting the Fire

Don't use a petroleum-based fire starter. It will ruin your meat—you'll be able to taste the chemicals. Any number of paraffin-coated wood shaving or fiberboard products on the market are far safer to use than liquids. The only exception is an alcohol gel product, most often found in woodstove stores. An electric element starter is also acceptable, if you have an electrical outlet nearby.

Mound up the briquets into a pile in either the charcoal chimney or barbecue unit. You will know the coals are ready when the briquets turn ash gray in color. Spread them out, put your waterpan below where your meat will be placed on the grid, and begin cooking.

Time and Temperature

You truly cannot rush good barbecue. Take into account these factors: the weight of the meat, the outside temperature, and the pit cooking temperature. When it's hot outside, the warm air will allow the meat to cook more quickly. When it's cold, the opposite is true. Whenever you take the lid off or open up your pit, you lose valuable heat and add more cooking time to the process.

One tip for testing the accuracy of your thermometer is to boil some water in a pan. Allow the water to come to a rolling boil, then place the thermometer into the pan. The temperature of the water should read 212°F. If your thermometer reads 207°F, you know that it's off by five degrees. This will help you gauge the exact temperature of your fire.

Mastering the skills that produce great barbecue and grilled foods takes time. It's not an overnight process. Write down everything you do. Have a game plan, then proceed. Pay attention to what is happening with your grill or pit, especially if you are working with an unfamiliar one.

Tools for Making Your Sauce

Food Processor

This versatile appliance works faster than a blender. With most processors, you can add ingredients while the machine is running. (Try the same thing in a blender and have fun doing lots of cleaning up!)

Saucepans

Most kitchenware experts recommend the use of either heavy-duty enamel or stainless steel pans in several sizes with lids. Avoid using aluminum which will react adversely to highly acidic content of tomatoes, mustards, fruits, and vinegars. Cheap, thin metal pans are notorious for having hot spots, which scorch food or heat unevenly.

Knives

The best quality steel knife you can purchase is the hot-dropped, forged, and ice-hardened carbon steel variety. This type of knife holds its sharpness extremely well. If a carbon steel knife is too expensive for your budget, a well-made stainless steel knife is your next best choice. Purchase plastic guards to protect the blades. A steel for sharpening knives is also a very good investment. My wife Sandi and I have our knives routinely sharpened twice a year by a local cutlery store.

Cutting Board

A cutting board is essential. There has been a lot of discussion in the food safety industry lately about wood versus polyethylene boards. Some people now recommend wood over plastic. Wood boards should be routinely sanded and oiled.

Poly boards are easier to maintain and clean than the wooden ones. In fact, many of the cookoffs that Sandi and I attend require that only poly boards be used by the contestants for cutting their meats. Should your poly board become stained by tomato paste or paprika, place it in a sink or tub filled with hot water and a capful of bleach, and let it sit for a few minutes; rinse it off carefully and it will look as good as new.

Other Kitchen Tools

You'll also wind up using plastic measuring spoons, glass or plastic measuring cups, a food mill, strainer, colander, sieve, slotted spoons (preferably food-grade plastic), grater, ginger grater, citrus zester, garlic press, pastry brushes, various sizes of nylon whisks, spatulas, and a sauce mop. These items are relatively inexpensive and may be purchased at most stores. There are also a number of mail-order catalogs that feature a wide assortment of gourmet kitchen tools and items.

Ingredients of Sauces

Spices and Herbs

Nothing can surpass the flavor of using the very freshest herbs and spices in your barbecue sauces. Carolyn Pervine of Captain Albert Goodthings in Salem, Oregon, advises that spices found in supermarket bulk food sections and in health food stores are much fresher than prepackaged spices, which often are stored in warehouses for months at a time. Air, light, and heat will rob spices and herbs of their essential oils. And once the package is opened, spices quickly lose their freshness. It is best to store herbs and spices in airtight, opaque glass jars, or in airtight, snap-lid containers. Once opened, keep your spices in a cool, dark spot to preserve and retain freshness.

Ann Wilder of Vann's Spices in Baltimore, Maryland, tells me that whole herbs and spices will stay fresh for up to a year if you put them into an airtight plastic bag and store them in the freezer. Ground herbs and spices will generally remain at their flavorful best for about three months. To enjoy maximum flavor from any herb or spice, grind the spice or herb as needed. An inexpensive way to do this is with a coffee grinder, which retails for around fifteen dollars. These little appliances do an excellent job of grinding herbs and spices. If you use the grinder for coffee, consider purchasing a separate grinder for hot pepper spices and herbs, or you'll really wind up with hot coffee! Whatever you do, wipe out the grinding chamber thoroughly after each use, or unplug the grinder and gently rinse it out with a sponge dipped in hot water and wrung out. Do not immerse the appliance in water.

There are two tests to tell if the spices you buy are fresh. How does it smell? Herbs and spices should give off a very pronounced aroma, easily discerned by your nose. How does it look? The plant or powder should have bright color. If it is pale and the aroma is scant, find another source of supply.

Liquids

Liquids of all kinds are used in making sauces. Name any potable liquid and I'll guarantee it has been tried in a sauce by someone. Here is a list of liquids successfully used in making barbecue sauces.

Ale/Beer

I have used both ale and beer as flavoring agents in sauces and marinades. Ales tend to be darker and denser in flavor, due to the amount of yeast used in the fermentation process. Allow the head to dissipate before mixing in additional ingredients. Regional microbrews tend to be fresher than the national brands. The fruit-flavored microbrews add unique flavor and another dimension to sauces and marinades.

Light and dark beers and nonalcoholic types can be used in sauce making. The beers with alcohol content tend to have a more balanced flavor and the alcohol burns off if you simmer the sauce or marinade, or use it as a basting liquid.

Coffee

A good number of flavorful sauces and marinades include brewed coffee. Go for quality by using whole beans, and grind them just prior to brewing. Dark roasted coffee beans have more surface carmelization and therefore exhibit a sharper, more pronounced flavor. I do not recommend flavored coffees; the flavoring can react unfavorably with other ingredients in your barbecue sauce.

Citrus Juices

Highly acidic and tart in flavor, citrus juices are wonderful liquids to use in both sauces and marinades. Take the extra time to squeeze fresh juice from limes, lemons, and oranges. Strain the juice to eliminate seeds, pulp, and other solid materials. Lime juice and mustard make a wonderful coating for pork. With lemons, look for fruit without any green color on the peel, which indicates that the lemons were not allowed to ripen. With limes, the darker the peel, the better. The Seville variety of oranges are considered the best for cooking.

Fruit Juices

Fruit juices other than citrus juices tend to be sweetened and easily burn when exposed to fire or high heat. Many commercial brands are made from very little real fruit, so read the labels carefully to see exactly what you are buying. Frozen concentrates such as Mango/Passion Fruit and other flavors can add an exotic taste to sauces and marinades. However, they also are highly sweetened.

Liquor

Bourbon, rum, and sour mash whiskey are all great sauce-enhancing liquids. The alcohol burns off in the cooking process, leaving the subtle flavor of the liquor behind. Liquor is an especially good ingredient to add to yellow prepared mustard, one of my favorite ways to flavor spareribs and pork tenderloin. Whiskey is good to add to glazes on meat for both color and flavor.

A couple of years ago, my wife and I attended spring training for competition barbecuers in Gig Harbor, Washington. Our friends from Seattle, the multi-award-winning Beaver Castors Cooking Team, used a mixture of rum and cola to flavor a leg of lamb and won first place in the category. Just about anything is fair game when developing a barbecue sauce. You are limited only by your imagination.

Oil

Oil is to replace moisture in meat that was lost through the introduction of acidic ingredients. Neutral oils, such as grapeseed, canola, or sunflower, are your best bets if you don't want to taint the flavor of the aromatics you are using. Jim Tarantino, in his book *Marinades* (The Crossing Press), cautions against the overuse of sesame and olive oils, which can overpower or flatten the flavor of sauces.

Soda Pop

Cola, cream soda, and root beer have found their way into more than one sauce or marinade. Like fruit juices, soda pop is highly sweetened and tends to burn when exposed to heat or prolonged cooking. If you are going to use soda pop, stay away from the diet varieties, because artificial sweetener leaves a bitter aftertaste when exposed to high levels of heat.

Soy Sauce

True Japanese soy sauce is a fermented liquid, made from wheat, salt, and soybeans. It is superior in flavor to its American counterpart, which tends to be loaded with salt, chemicals, and preservatives. Health food stores generally will sell Asian bottled soy sauce and bulk Shoyu sauce, a high-quality product. Taste both to see what kind you like and check the label to see if any chemical additives or preservatives are in the sauce.

Vinegar

A primary ingredient in many barbecue sauces in the Deep South, vinegar adds tartness. Cider vinegar works well with beef and pork, but overpowers fish. Balsamic and wine vinegars are aged in wooden barrels and have less of an edge than other varieties. White wine vinegars or champagne vinegars are particularly good with fish.

Wine

Most cooks I've talked to agree that you don't need to use expensive wine. Rieslings, ports, and sherries are all good varieties with which to experiment. You would do well to avoid white zinfandels and blush wines which typically do not add an agreeable flavor to sauces or marinades.

Water

Good old H_2O is a valuable ingredient, especially if you need to thin out the sauce a little, or dilute the other ingredients. Those of you who live in areas where the water is heavily chlorinated should use spring or distilled water so you don't ruin the flavor of your sauce or have it turn out smelling like the community swimming pool.

Worcestershire Sauce

A staple of many Southern-style sauces, this liquid turns everything dark, dark, dark! Worcestershire sauce also contains those salty anchovies. Keep that in mind if you plan on adding salt to your sauce recipe.

Sweeteners

Honey/Maple Syrup

Either natural ingredient can be used as a sweetener and flavoring agent. They also counteract highly acidic ingredients and tend to combine with liquids more easily than granulated sugar. Honey, cup for cup, is twenty-five percent sweeter than granulated sugar. Take that into account when using it as a sauce ingredient or as a substitute for sugar. Maple syrup is thiry percent sweeter than sugar. Approximately one pint of maple syrup is equivalent to one pound of granulated sugar.

Jellies

A great way to add fruity flavor to sauces, and to sweeten and thicken them, is by using jellies. Unlike jams,* which contain fruit solids, jellies melt easily into liquid. One cautionary note: most commercially produced jellies have a fifty-five percent sugar content. Due to the high amount of sugar, use a jelly-based mixture only as a finishing sauce.

Molasses

A byproduct of sun-ripened sugar cane, molasses is not as sweet as its cousin, sugar. For cooking purposes, use unsulfured molasses or the light-colored variety. Blackstrap molasses should be avoided, as it is the final byproduct of further boiling of the sugar cane, and has a rather unpleasant taste.

*You can use jam for sweetening your sauce if you are going to strain the sauce later to get the seeds out.

The Eight Commandments

Now we're ready to begin, right? Not yet! Some barbecue sauce basics should be covered first. These recipes are a very good basic education. Once you are comfortable making various types of sauces, you'll probably want to concoct your own, and you should. However, every aspiring sauce inventor should follow these sauce commandments.

1. Follow directions to the letter. If the recipe calls for a certain ingredient, don't ignore it (at least the first couple of times you use it). The people who have developed these sauces have used these specific ingredients in the recipe.
2. Use accurate measurements. I know firsthand the temptation to add just a pinch of that and a dollop of this when making sauces. But how can you recreate a sauce masterpiece if you don't measure the ingredients as you go?
3. Always use the freshest ingredients possible. You'll wind up with better-tasting sauces. It never pays to cut corners on your ingredients.
4. Strive for balance in all things. If you are using pungent woods, such as hickory, mesquite, oak, or pecan in your barbecuing or grilling, you'll have better results using a lighter-flavored sauce than one that will compete with the meat and smoke. Too many conflicting tastes will ultimately ruin your hard work.
5. Remember that sauces are meant to complement your cooking, not hide it. View barbecue sauces as condiments, the same way mustard and ketchup enhance a hot dog. Barbecue sauce should help draw out the flavor of your barbecued and grilled meats, not overpower it.
6. Write everything down! You'll be thinking up all sorts of interesting combinations of liquids, spices, herbs, and flavors, and mixing up one heck of a recipe, but when you want to recreate it later you will forget how you did it! Don't waste that precious culinary inspiration. Write down exactly what you do every time you make up a new sauce. Your creation could become the next big seller!
7. Experiment. Hey, variety is the spice of life! You'd be surprised how a little experimentation can lead to a truly tasty discovery in the kitchen.
8. Most of all, have fun! Cooking is an activity you can enjoy by yourself or with friends and family. Nothing brings more people together with big, happy smiles than well-prepared barbecue, complemented by a sauce you've made from scratch.

Sweet Sauces

*S*ugars, honey, molasses, jellies, soda pop, fruit juices, and other sweeteners are the foundation for this group of sauces. Most barbecuers and grillers at one time or another have put a sugar-rich barbecue sauce on their meat and, horrified, watched it burn. That can happen if you aren't careful. To avoid burning the meat you can use the indirect-fire method of cooking.

Adding liquid ingredients to honey, such as bourbon or sour mash whiskey, helps to produce a distinctive, sweet finish to your barbecuing and grilling. Try mixing in a little cayenne pepper to give the honey some heat. I often use warm honey as a finishing glaze when cooking ribs. It gives them a brilliant sheen and just the right touch of sweetness.

Exotic fruit juices are a welcome addition to sweet barbecue sauces. Most contain high amounts of sweeteners; keep that in mind before adding more sweetener to the recipe.

Dissolved fruit jellies and marmalades can be used, providing an exotic or fruity taste to your sauces. Sweet sauces aren't meant to be candy sweet—they are meant to complement, not compete with, the flavor of the meat.

Sweet sauces go best with pork, seafood, and chicken. Personally, I don't recommend a sweet sauce for beef, unless you are preparing an Oriental barbecue dish.

Overleaf: Canadian barbecuer Brad Bradfield's VW bus cooker; Campbell's Bar-B-Q in Portland, Oregon.

Apricot Sweet 'n' Sour Sauce

This was one of those experimental sauces that came from an exploration of the kitchen cabinet. Try this kind of exploration in your home; you might be surprised at what you come up with.

1/2 cup dried apricots
1 1/2 cups water
1 shallot, minced
3 tablespoons vegetable oil
1/2 cup white wine vinegar
1/4 cup honey
1/2 teaspoon soy sauce
1/4 cup ketchup
1/2 teaspoon oregano
1/2 teaspoon tarragon
1/2 teaspoon salt
1/4 teaspoon freshly ground pepper

Combine apricots with water in a small saucepan. Heat to boiling; reduce heat. Simmer, uncovered, until tender, about 30 minutes. Cool slightly.

Place the apricots with the liquid (about 1/2 cup) in a food processor or blender. Process until smooth. Transfer to a medium saucepan; add remaining ingredients. Boil the sauce briefly.

Yield: 3 cups

Apricot-Pineapple Sauce

The apricots and pineapple join to make this a slightly tart, sweet sauce. Pork and turkey work well with it.

1 medium onion, diced
1 cup dried apricots, chopped
1/2 cup pineapple juice
3 to 4 cloves garlic, minced
1 tablespoon minced ginger
1 tablespoon Dijon-style mustard
1 cup cider vinegar
2 tablespoons Worcestershire sauce
2 tablespoons tomato purée
1/3 cup firmly packed brown sugar
1 teaspoon freshly ground pepper
1/4 teaspoon allspice
1/2 teaspoon salt

Combine all the ingredients in a saucepan. Simmer over medium heat 20 to 25 minutes, stirring occasionally. Allow to cool, then transfer to a food processor fitted with a steel blade. Process 15 to 20 seconds.

Yield: 1 1/2 cups

Guava Barbecue Sauce

Virtually any tropical fruit can work well in this sauce. Be daring and experiment with mango or papaya pulp. Guava paste can be found in Latin markets. Incidentally, the mixture of guava, cider vinegar, dark rum, and tomato paste is extraordinary—really pleasing to the palate.

1 cup guava paste

6 tablespoons cider vinegar

1/4 cup dark rum

1/4 cup tomato paste

1/4 cup fresh lime juice

1 tablespoon soy sauce

2 teaspoons ketchup

2 teaspoons Worcestershire sauce

2 tablespoons minced onion

1 tablespoon minced ginger

2 cloves garlic, minced

1/4 to 1/2 scotch bonnet or other hot chile, seeded and minced

Salt and freshly ground pepper, to taste

In a mixing bowl thoroughly combine all ingredients.

Yield: 2 1/2 cups

Last Mango in Paris Barbecue Sauce

With apologies or thanks to Chief Parrothead, Jimmy Buffett, whose song "Last Mango in Paris" helped solve the dilemma of this title.

2 tablespoons olive oil

1 medium onion, chopped

1 medium red bell pepper, chopped

1 teaspoon salt

1/3 cup red wine vinegar

3 tablespoons molasses

2 tablespoons soy sauce

1/4 teaspoon allspice

1 medium ripe mango (about 1 pound), peeled, seeded, cut into chunks

3 fresh jalapeños, seeded, in chunks

In a skillet, heat oil over moderate heat. Add onion and bell pepper with salt until softened. Stir in vinegar, molasses, soy sauce, and allspice; bring to a boil. Simmer mixture 1 minute to blend flavors. Let cool slightly. Pour mixture into a blender; add mango and jalapeños and blend until smooth. You can decrease or increase the number of jalapeños if you like less or more heat in your sauce.

Yield: 1 1/2 cups

Orangy-Tangy Barbecue Sauce

The inspiration for this sauce comes from watching Clyde, the orangutan in Clint Eastwood's Every Which Way *series of movies. I picture Clyde as somewhat simplified in his cooking approach but adventurous in his choice of ingredients. Try "monkeying" around with this recipe—your friends will go "ape" over the results!*

3/4 cup chili sauce

1/4 cup soy sauce

2 tablespoons red wine vinegar

1/2 teaspoon grated ginger

1/4 cup fresh orange juice

1 teaspoon minced orange zest

1/4 cup molasses

2 tablespoons minced onion

2 teaspoons Tabasco

Combine all ingredients in a large saucepan. Stir to blend; bring to boil. Let it cool.

Yield: 1 1/4 cups

SAUCEMASTER TIP

Need a thicker sauce? A teaspoon or two of cornstarch dissolved in a bit of cold water will usually do the trick in a jiffy.

Key West Barbecue Sauce

Way down there at the tip of the Southeastern United States one of the major events of the day is watching the sunset. I believe that with that kind of attitude, "Conchs," as the locals are called, would make great barbecuers. It takes real patience to make great barbecue.

1 tablespoon vegetable oil

1 large onion, minced

1/4 teaspoon red pepper flakes

1/2 cup fresh key lime juice*

2 tablespoons fresh lemon juice

1 teaspoon salt

1 tablespoon seeded and minced jalapeño

1 dried ancho chile, reconstituted, seeded, and finely chopped

1 cup fresh orange juice

2 tablespoons sugar

1 tablespoon chopped cilantro

In a saucepan over medium heat, add oil and sauté the onion and red pepper flakes until onions are soft. Add remaining ingredients and bring to a boil. Reduce heat and stir frequently, until sauce thickens slightly.

Yield: 2 1/2 cups

*If you can't find key limes, use Persian limes (the kind available in most groceries).

Georgia Peach Sauce

This is a fine, summertime sauce that calls for the sweetest, ripest peaches you can find. I am fond of using this on lighter meats such as a pork tenderloin.

3 ripe peaches, peeled and sliced
1/4 cup raisins
1 cup fresh orange juice
3 tablespoons sugar
2 tablespoons grated ginger
1/4 cup cider vinegar
2 tablespoons fresh lemon juice
1/4 cup soy sauce

Purée the peaches and raisins in a food processor or blender. Transfer to a small bowl, add all the remaining ingredients, and stir until smooth.

Yield: 2 cups

Pineapple Marinade

My friend Dennis Hayes first tasted this while in the Caribbean and managed to pry the recipe from a chef at a beachside restaurant in St. John, in the Virgin Islands. This works best on chicken and seafood.

1 cup pineapple juice
1/3 cup soy sauce
1 tablespoon chopped cilantro
  or Italian parsley
1/4 cup dry white wine
1/4 cup crushed pineapple
1 tablespoon honey
cayenne

Thoroughly combine all ingredients. Adjust the cayenne to your taste.

Yield: 2 cups

SAUCEMASTER TIP

Honey, by itself, is an excellent finishing glaze for pork spareribs. Simply warm the honey in your pit during the final ten minutes of cooking and lightly brush it over the ribs with a pastry brush. The ribs will shine brilliantly and have a subtle, sweet taste.

Plum Ginger Barbecue Sauce

The combination of plums and ginger is plum brilliant.

4 dark plums (about 3/4 pound), peeled, pitted and cut into 1-inch pieces
1 tablespoon finely grated ginger
1 clove garlic, chopped
3 tablespoons hoisin sauce
2 tablespoons firmly packed brown sugar
2 tablespoons soy sauce
1 tablespoon cider vinegar
4 tablespoons chopped chives

In a saucepan, simmer all the ingredients except vinegar and chives. Cover and stir occasionally until the plums fall apart, about 20 minutes. Add vinegar and simmer, uncovered, stirring frequently, until sauce is the consistency of ketchup, about 10 minutes. Stir in chives.

Yield: 1 1/4 cups

Homemade Plum Sauce

What to do with those overripe plums? Make this nice finishing sauce for pork, turkey, or chicken.

6 ripe plums, peeled and seeded
1/4 cup white wine vinegar
1/2 cup water
1/3 cup pineapple juice
1/4 cup sugar
2 tablespoons soy sauce
2 cloves garlic, minced

In a saucepan, mix all ingredients and bring to a boil; reduce heat and simmer 30 minutes. Allow to cool. Purée in a blender until smooth.

Yield: 1 1/2 cups

Cardinal barbecue rule number one: Write everything down every time you prepare to cook barbecue!

—Paul Kirk, Kansas City Baron of Barbecue

Florida Sunshine Sauce

If the tomato is the star in most barbecue sauces, the orange deserves an award for best supporting role. Use this sauce as a basting or dipping sauce; it also makes a nice marinade for poultry or seafood.

1 cup fresh orange juice

4 ounces chili sauce

1/4 cup soy sauce

1/4 cup molasses

2 tablespoons white vinegar

2 tablespoons grated onion

1/2 teaspoon grated ginger

2 teaspoons hot pepper sauce

Combine all ingredients in a large saucepan. Stir to blend, then bring to a boil and let cool.

Yield: 1 1/2 cups

Mandarin Orange Sauce

Tangerines can also be used in this recipe. Increase the sugar to taste. Use this as a glaze or as a finishing sauce for chicken or pork.

1 can (11 ounces) mandarin orange segments, with liquid

3 tablespoons unsalted butter

2 shallots, minced

1/4 cup chicken broth

1/4 teaspoon salt

1/2 teaspoon minced orange peel

3 tablespoons sugar

In a saucepan, combine all ingredients and heat until just starting to boil. Remove from heat and purée in a blender until smooth.

Yield: 1 3/4 cups

Que is what they call it in Georgia, where it has been famous for many, many years. Boston has its pork and beans, but Georgia has its barbecue which beats them all.

—John Watkins, *Stands Magazine*, London, 1898, quoted in John Egerton's *Southern Food*

Raspberry Basting Sauce

You can use fresh raspberries for this sauce. Just cook the raspberries with a little sugar and strain out the seeds. I've tried both strawberries and blackberries instead of raspberries and wasn't as pleased with the results.

1 jar (12 ounces) raspberry preserves
3 tablespoons red wine vinegar
1/2 cup ketchup
1 teaspoon chile powder
1 teaspoon Dijon mustard

Strain preserves through a sieve into a medium saucepan. Pour vinegar through the sieve to loosen the seeds. Discard seeds. Add ketchup, chile powder, and mustard to the saucepan. Heat to boiling; reduce heat. Simmer 2 minutes.

Yield: 2 1/4 cups

Tangerine-Tamarind Sauce

Tamarind shows up in a number of Asian, Mexican, and Caribbean recipes. When paired with tangerines it yields a crisp, sweet/tart sauce that is excellent on turkey.

1 cup white vinegar
1/3 cup sugar
Peels of 3 tangerines
1 tablespoon minced ginger
Juice of 10 tangerines
1 tablespoon tamarind paste

In a saucepan, bring vinegar and sugar to a boil. Add tangerine peels and ginger, and simmer until the liquid is reduced by half, about 15 minutes. Remove from heat, strain liquid into a bowl, and discard the peels and ginger.

Return liquid to the saucepan, add tangerine juice and tamarind paste, bring to a simmer, and reduce the liquid volume by half to a third, about 20 minutes. Remove sauce from heat and allow to cool to room temperature. This sauce keeps well, covered and refrigerated, up to 2 weeks.

Yield: 1 1/2 cups

Pacific Rim Barbecue Sauce

There are a lot of flavors in this sauce; the toasted sesame oil is what makes it work. Use as a finishing or dipping sauce.

Peel of 1/4 orange, grated
1 clove garlic, minced
1 tablespoon toasted sesame oil
1/4 cup red wine vinegar
1/4 cup rice wine vinegar
3/4 cup pineapple juice
1/4 cup firmly packed dark brown sugar
1/4 cup ketchup
1 tablespoon soy sauce
1 tablespoon chopped cilantro
1 tablespoon cornstarch
1/8 cup cold water

Sauté the orange peel and garlic in sesame oil 3 to 4 minutes. Add all remaining ingredients, except cornstarch and water. Bring to a boil. Mix the cornstarch and water. Add mixture slowly, stirring until it thickens. Remove from heat. Let cool to room temperature.

Yield: 2 cups

Firehouse Barbecue Sauce

Firefighters are some of our country's finest impromptu cooks. An upstate New York fireman gave me his recipe for barbecue sauce, but would not reveal his tuna noodle casserole recipe.

3 tablespoons orange marmalade
1/4 cup olive oil
1/2 cup dry red wine
1 1/2 cups ketchup
1/4 cup firmly packed dark brown sugar
2 scallions, sliced paper thin, crosswise
4 cloves garlic, pressed
1 tablespoon grated ginger
1 tablespoon soy sauce
1/4 cup water
2 tablespoons red chile powder
Juice and zest of 1 lemon
1/4 cup minced parsley

Combine all ingredients in a stainless steel bowl; blend well. Let sit overnight, refrigerated, to allow the flavors to merge.

Yield: 3 cups

Santa Fe Chile Barbecue Sauce

This barbecue sauce has the flavor and aroma of sweet red New Mexican chiles and the slight, smoky-hot flavor of chipotles. Honey and malt extract are used here for sweet flavor and sticky texture. Cider vinegar adds tartness, balancing the other flavors. Use this as a finishing sauce or a mop.

2 New Mexican dried chiles

6 sun-dried tomato halves

1 small can (4 to 6 ounces) chipotles

2 cloves garlic

1 medium onion, sliced

1 scallion, chopped

1 teaspoon oregano

1/2 bottle (6 ounces) dark beer

1 teaspoon salt

1 cup cider vinegar

2 tablespoons soy sauce

1/2 cup honey

1/2 cup amber malt extract, or molasses

1 teaspoon lemon juice

Rehydrate the dried chiles and tomatoes in boiling water. Let them stand for 20 minutes. Drain. Reserve the soaking liquid. Slice the chiles and discard the seeds. Then add chipotles, garlic, onion, scallions, oregano, and beer. Purée in a blender until mixture is smooth. Add some of the water from the chile pepper rehydration. Continue blending for 30 seconds. Mix purée and the remaining ingredients in a saucepan. Bring to a low boil for about 5 minutes, then reduce heat to a simmer. Stir sauce frequently. When the mixture sticks to the stirring spoon without dripping, the sauce is done.

Yield: 3 cups

Dinosaur Bar B Que in Syracuse, New York

Deep South Cola Barbecue Sauce

2 tablespoons unsalted butter

1 onion, finely chopped

2 cloves garlic, minced

1 bay leaf, crumbled

2 cups ketchup

3/4 cup Coca-Cola

1 tablespoon Worcestershire sauce

1 teaspoon Dijon mustard

2 teaspoons red wine vinegar

Salt and freshly ground pepper, to taste

Allow the cola to turn flat (no carbonation present) before using it in the recipe. For some reason other colas don't work as well as Coca-Cola.

Melt butter in a medium saucepan over medium-low heat. Add onion; cook 1 minute. Add garlic; cook 4 minutes longer. Do not brown. Stir in remaining ingredients. Heat to boiling; reduce heat. Simmer, uncovered, stirring occasionally, 1 hour.

Yield: 2 cups

Lola's Cola Sauce

This is another variation on the many Southern sauce recipes that call for cola. Remember to let the Coca-Cola go flat.

3/4 cup Coca-Cola

3/4 cup ketchup

2 tablespoons white vinegar

2 tablespoons A-1 sauce

1/2 teaspoon chile powder

1/2 teaspoon salt

Combine ingredients in a saucepan and bring to a boil. Reduce heat and simmer, covered, about 30 minutes, or until sauce is very thick. Stir frequently.

Yield: 2 cups

SAUCEMASTER TIP

If you're using soda pop as a liquid ingredient for your sauces, don't use the diet varieties. The artificial sweetener turns bitter once the soda has been exposed to high heat. It will spoil the flavor of your sauce and meat.

Naw'lins Barbecue Sauce

This spicy blend goes well with barbecued shrimp. Baste them with the sauce and set some aside for dipping.

1/2 cup ketchup
1/2 cup tomato paste
1/4 cup currant jelly
1/8 cup Dijon mustard
1/4 cup firmly packed brown sugar
1/4 cup red wine vinegar
2 tablespoons bourbon whiskey
1 tablespoon Worcestershire sauce
1 tablespoon A-1 sauce
1 tablespoon Cajun spice blend
1 teaspoon dry mustard
2 tablespoons honey
1/2 teaspoon coarsely cracked pepper
Salt, to taste

Combine all ingredients and blend well.

Yield: 2 1/2 cups

Whiskey Town BBQ Sauce

Here is another fine example of Jack Daniels's contribution to the barbecue world.

1/2 medium onion, finely chopped
2 cloves garlic, minced
1/2 cup Jack Daniels
1 cup ketchup
1/3 cup cider vinegar
1/4 cup Worcestershire sauce
1/3 teaspoon Tabasco, to taste
1/4 cup molasses
1/2 teaspoon pepper
1/2 tablespoon salt
1/4 cup tomato paste
2 tablespoons liquid smoke
1/4 cup firmly packed brown sugar

Combine onion, garlic, and Jack Daniels in a saucepan. Sauté until onion and garlic are soft, approximately 10 minutes. Add remaining ingredients. Bring to boil; reduce heat. Simmer, uncovered, 20 minutes, stirring constantly. Strain the mixture if you prefer a smoother sauce.

Yield: 2 1/2 cups

Hard Stuff Barbecue Sauce

This recipe is simple—six ingredients in all—but very tasty.

3/4 cup ketchup
1/2 cup maple syrup
1/4 cup vegetable oil
1/4 cup bourbon
2 tablespoons cider vinegar
2 tablespoons Dijon mustard

In a medium bowl, combine all ingredients. Whisk to blend well.

Yield: 1 3/4 cups

A Taste of Vermont Sopping Syrup

This sauce may be a bit sweeter than most people are used to, but it is quite tasty and the ingredients are balanced nicely. Try it as a finishing sauce for barbecued chicken breasts.

2 tablespoons unsalted butter
1 tablespoon dry mustard
1/2 cup maple syrup
3/4 cup ketchup
1/2 cup cider vinegar
1 teaspoon crushed celery seeds
1/2 teaspoon chile powder
1 teaspoon cayenne
1/2 teaspoon salt

Combine all ingredients in a medium saucepan. Heat to boiling; reduce heat. Simmer, uncovered, for 20 minutes.

Yield: 2 cups

Corky's Bar-B-Q in Memphis, Tennessee

Savory Sauces

rom the sublime to the stupendous, these savory barbecue sauces swirl with herbs and spices. You will find a wide range of palate-pleasers in this chapter, quite versatile with all types of meat or fish.

My friend Remus Powers, that "ole saucemeister" from Kansas City, cautions against getting too rambunctious or heavy-handed with herbs and spices. If you use fresh herbs, they contain more of their essential oils and are more intense in flavor than dried herbs. Some of these recipes yield a large quantity of sauce. Most of them, because of their vinegar content, will store well, covered, in the refrigerator.

Overleaf: Bell's Bar-B-Q in Syracuse, New York; Bruce Bjorkman; the world's largest pit owned by Kraft.

Carolina Spicy Vinegar Marinade

In the Carolinas the debate rages on. Tomato or vinegar base? It may take several tastings to decide—Yum!

1 cup red wine vinegar

1 cup water

1 onion, thinly sliced

2 cloves garlic, minced

6 sprigs parsley

2 bay leaves

2 ribs celery with leaves, coarsely chopped

2 juniper berries, crushed

1 teaspoon chopped thyme,
   or 1/2 teaspoon dried

1 teaspoon chopped rosemary,
   or 1/2 teaspoon dried

1 teaspoon chopped basil,
   or 1/2 teaspoon dried

1 tablespoon firmly packed dark
   brown sugar

Combine all ingredients in a bowl. Let stand 30 minutes or longer to let the flavors blend. This may be used as a marinade and/or a basting sauce.

Yield: 3 1/2 cups

Eastern North Carolina-style Sauce

1 cup white vinegar

1 cup cider vinegar

1 tablespoon sugar

1 tablespoon red pepper flakes

1 tablespoon Tabasco

Salt and freshly cracked pepper,
   to taste

Mix together. Let stand 30 minutes or so to let the flavors blend.

Yield: 2 cups

The Sweet Taste of Sauce-cess

Back in 1983, Ardie Davis (aka Remus Powers) started the Diddy-Wa-Diddy sauce contest on his backyard patio. Today, it is the largest commercial sauce contest of its type in the world, averaging four hundred sauce entries each year.

Eastern Carolina Hot Vinegar Barbecue Sauce

Bring up the topic of barbecue sauces in the Carolinas and it's likely to escalate into another go-round of the Hatfields and McCoys! One thing's for sure, these tangy and hot regional sauces are worth fighting over.

2 cups cider vinegar
1 tablespoon crushed red pepper flakes
Salt and pepper, to taste

Mix together all the ingredients.

Yield: 2 cups

Piedmont-Lexington-style Sauce

1 1/2 cups white vinegar
1/2 cup ketchup
Salt, to taste
1/2 teaspoon cayenne
1/2 teaspoon crushed red pepper flakes
1 tablespoon sugar
1/2 cup water

Combine all ingredients in a saucepan and bring to a simmer. Cook, stirring, until the sugar dissolves. Remove from heat and let stand until cool.

Yield: 3 cups

Campbell's Bar-B-Q in Portland, Oregon

Texas-style BBQ Sauce

This BIG batch from the Lone Star State is a good way to feed a large barbecue gathering. It works exceptionally well on beef and pork.

1/2 pound pickling spices
1 teaspoon whole cloves
1 medium onion, chopped
2 stalks celery, chopped
36 ounces ketchup
1/2 cup chili sauce
1 quart water
1/2 cup cider vinegar
1 tablespoon dry mustard
1/2 cup Worcestershire sauce
1/2 cup firmly packed light brown sugar
1/4 tablespoon garlic powder
1 tablespoon salt, to taste
1 tablespoon Tabasco
2 tablespoons lemon juice

Tie pickling spices and cloves loosely in cheesecloth bag. Combine all ingredients in a heavy pot; heat to a boil. Reduce heat and simmer slowly, about 1 1/2 hours. Remove from heat; cool partially. Remove spice bag. Pour mixture into blender and blend until smooth. Cover until ready to serve.

Yield: 2 quarts

Texas Hill Country Soppin' Sauce

The hill country around Austin, Texas, is truly beautiful, a blessed piece of earth. While most Texas barbecues don't call for a basting sauce, this version is as at home on the table as it is on the meat.

2 cloves garlic, chopped
1 tablespoon red pepper flakes
1/2 teaspoon chopped cilantro
1/4 teaspoon cumin
1/2 teaspoon anise seeds
1/2 teaspoon salt
2 tablespoons firmly packed brown sugar
1 tablespoon Worcestershire sauce
1 cup cider vinegar
2 cups ketchup
Hot pepper sauce, to taste

Combine all ingredients except ketchup and hot pepper sauce in a blender or food processor. Process until smooth. Transfer the mixture to a saucepan and add ketchup. Heat to boiling; reduce heat. Simmer, uncovered, 30 minutes. Add the hot pepper sauce to taste.

Yield: 3 cups

Rib Stickin' Sauce

Whether you're a fan of pork or beef ribs, this sauce is sure to satisfy.

2 tablespoons unsalted butter

1 onion, minced

2 cloves garlic, minced

Juice of 1 orange

1 tablespoon raisins

2 tablespoons cider vinegar

2 tablespoons vegetable oil

Grated rind of 1 orange

1 cup molasses

1 cup ketchup

2 teaspoons chile powder

Pinch ground cloves

1 teaspoon Dijon mustard

1 teaspoon Worcestershire sauce

2 teaspoons crushed red pepper flakes

1/2 teaspoon salt

Melt butter in a medium saucepan over medium-low heat. Add onion; cook 1 minute. Add garlic and cook 4 minutes. Be careful not to brown the garlic. Meanwhile, combine the orange juice with the raisins, vinegar, and oil in a food processor or blender. Process until smooth. Add this mixture, along with the remaining ingredients, to the saucepan. Heat to boiling; reduce heat. Simmer, uncovered, 15 minutes.

Yield: 3 cups

Chipotle-Molasses Glaze

The smokiness of the chipotle peppers, increasingly available in supermarkets, is a formidable companion to the molasses for a rich glaze that works nicely on beef.

1 cup white vinegar

4 tablespoons sugar

1 cup fresh orange juice

4 tablespoons molasses

6 canned chipotles, puréed

4 tablespoons chopped cilantro

Salt and freshly ground pepper, to taste

Juice of 2 limes

Combine the vinegar and sugar in a saucepan, bring to a boil, and simmer until reduced in volume by half, about 10 minutes. Add orange juice and again simmer until reduced in volume by half, another 10 minutes. Remove from heat; add molasses, chipotle, and cilantro. Stir well. Season with salt and pepper to taste, and finish by adding lime juice and mixing well.

Yield: 1 cup

Barbecue Sauce

This sauce is good for basting, best for poultry. It makes enough sauce for 10 broiler halves, weighing about 1 pound each. To reduce quantity, divide ingredients by two, except use a whole egg and 2 teaspoons of salt.

1 egg
1 cup vegetable oil
1 pint cider vinegar
1 tablespoon salt
1 tablespoon poultry seasoning
1 teaspoon pepper

Beat the egg, add oil, and beat again. Add remaining ingredients and stir. Brush sauce on chicken every few minutes.

Yield: 3 cups

Mel's Moppin' Sauce

1 cup cider vinegar
5 tablespoons Worcestershire sauce
2/3 cup vegetable oil
3 tablespoons butter
1 lemon, thinly sliced, with peel on
2 to 3 cloves garlic, minced
3 tablespoons grated ginger
2 tablespoons dry mustard

Combine all ingredients in a saucepan and heat until flavors are nicely blended, about 15 minutes. After it cools, strain the lemon slices out.

Yield: 2 cups

Chuckwagon BBQ Sauce

The key to this recipe is to keep of some of Cookie's gutgrinder coffee available. Toss a few of the grounds in for texture.

1/4 cup (1/2 stick) butter
2 cloves garlic, minced
1 onion, minced
1 carrot, grated
1/8 cup white vinegar
Juice of 1/2 lemon
1/4 cup Worcestershire sauce
1/3 cup firmly packed brown sugar
1/2 cup strong coffee, preferably from a weather-beaten, blackened campfire coffeepot
2 cups ketchup
2 tablespoons cayenne
2 tablespoons chile powder
2 teaspoons salt
2 teaspoons freshly ground pepper

Melt butter in a large saucepan; add garlic, onion, and carrot. Cook, stirring frequently, over low heat until tender, about 10 minutes. Add remaining ingredients and cook over medium heat, uncovered, until thickened, about 2 hours. Stir frequently.

Yield: 3 cups

Guasacaca

(Venezuela-style Barbecue Sauce)

Virtually all of the recipes for South American barbecue that I have come across called for beef. However, the sauces vary, calling for fruits, peppers, tomatoes, herbs, and vinegars. This is the only sauce I know of that uses avocado.

1/4 cup onion, minced

1 clove garlic, minced

1 habanero chile, seeds and stem removed, minced

1 large ripe Haas avocado, peeled, pit removed

1 cup peeled, chopped, ripe tomatoes

1/2 cup olive oil

1/8 cup red wine vinegar, or lime juice

1 teaspoon prepared mustard

1 tablespoon minced parsley

Salt, to taste

With a mortar and pestle, mash the onion, garlic, chile, avocado, and tomatoes into a paste. This may need to be done in batches. Add the remaining ingredients and blend well with a fork.

Yield: 2 cups

Creole Barbecue Sauce

When I was in Baton Rouge I ate at a roadside barbecue shack. The name escapes me. Later, I wrote down my guess at what I thought was in the sauce and have attempted to recreate it here.

2 tablespoons chile powder

1 tablespoon gumbo file—this dry spice blend is available in most supermarkets and is commonly used in many Cajun recipes

2 teaspoons dry mustard

1/3 cup red wine vinegar

1/2 cup olive oil

4 cloves garlic, minced

2 onions, minced

1/4 cup hearty red wine

3 tomatoes, seeded and minced

2 tablespoons minced Italian parsley

Salt, to taste

Combine the chile powder, gumbo file, and mustard with a little vinegar to make a paste. Add the rest of the vinegar and the olive oil and beat with a whisk. In a saucepan, heat a few tablespoons of olive oil and sauté the garlic and onion until slightly browned. Add the spice paste and remaining ingredients. Stir well and let sit, allowing the flavors to blend.

Yield: 3 cups

All-American Sauce

1 can (16 ounces) tomato sauce
2 tablespoons firmly packed brown sugar
1/4 cup vinegar
2 tablespoons Worcestershire sauce
1 teaspoon salt
1 tablespoon paprika
1 teaspoon dry mustard
1 teaspoon chile powder
2 tablespoons minced scallion
1/8 teaspoon cayenne

Put all the ingredients in a saucepan and simmer 15 minutes, stirring occasionally.

Yield: 2 1/2 cups

Sweet 'n' Savory Sauce

1/2 cup minced onion
1 can (6 ounces) tomato paste
3/4 cup water
4 tablespoons red wine vinegar
2 tablespoons firmly packed brown sugar
2 tablespoons Worcestershire sauce
2 tablespoons ketchup
1 teaspoon salt
1 teaspoon paprika
1 teaspoon chile powder
1/4 teaspoon pepper
1/4 teaspoon cinnamon
1/4 teaspoon cloves

Combine ingredients and simmer.

Yield: 2 cups

Flamin' Groovy Basting Sauce

During the 1960s and early '70s, the Flamin' Groovies were one of the many San Francisco-based psychedelic bands that emerged during the Summer of Love. I've always found their music inspiring and dedicate this sauce to them. This sauce is especially good on chicken and works well with pork also.

1 egg
1 cup vegetable oil
1 pint cider vinegar
3 tablespoons salt
1 tablespoon poultry seasoning
1 habanero chile, deveined, seeded, and chopped
1 teaspoon pepper

Beat the egg in a bowl, add oil, and beat again. Add remaining ingredients; transfer to a food processor and blend for 30 seconds.

Yield: 1 1/2 cups

All-American Mustard Sauce

Make ole man French proud—use his prepared yellow mustard for this South Carolina-inspired sauce. It makes a tangy baste for steak too.

1/2 cup sugar

1/4 teaspoon oregano

1/2 teaspoon thyme

1/2 teaspoon pepper

1/2 teaspoon cornstarch

1/8 teaspoon cayenne

1 teaspoon salt

1/2 cup cider vinegar

1 cup molasses

1 cup prepared mustard

1/2 cup ketchup

2 tablespoons vegetable oil

Combine the first seven ingredients in a small saucepan. Stir in enough vinegar to make a paste. Combine molasses, ketchup, mustard, oil, and remaining vinegar. Add to herb paste. Bring to a boil, stirring constantly. Reduce heat and simmer, uncovered, 10 minutes. Stir frequently.

Yield: 2 1/2 cups

Mushroom BBQ Sauce

Mushrooms are not one of the first ingredients that come to mind when discussing barbecue sauces. However, some mushrooms such as the shiitake add an earthy aroma and flavor to a sauce. Ordinary mushrooms, the brown or white variety, also taste good. This sauce works with any meat, especially lamb.

1/4 cup olive oil

1 cup fresh shiitake mushrooms, stems removed and discarded, finely chopped

6 cloves garlic, finely chopped

1 teaspoon chile powder

1 tablespoon dried basil

1 tablespoon dried oregano

2 tablespoons honey

1 can (16 ounces) tomato sauce

In a saucepan, heat the olive oil and sauté the mushrooms until they turn soft and give off their liquid. Add remaining ingredients and bring to a boil. Reduce heat and simmer 30 minutes.

Yield: 2 1/3 cups

Subtly Citrus Barbecue Sauce

This sauce has just the right blend of tanginess, slight heat, and pungency. I suggest trying it on a firm fish such as swordfish or halibut.

1 large white onion, minced

1 tablespoon red chile powder

1/4 teaspoon crushed red pepper flakes

1 ancho chile, seeded and finely chopped

1 tablespoon vegetable oil

1 cup orange or tangerine juice

2 tablespoons sugar

1/2 cup lime juice

2 tablespoons lemon juice

1 tablespoon chopped cilantro

1 teaspoon salt

Cook onion, red chile powder, red pepper flakes, and ancho chile in oil, stirring frequently until onion is tender, about 5 minutes. Stir in remaining ingredients. Heat to boil, then reduce heat to low. Simmer, uncovered, about 10 minutes, stirring occasionally.

Yield: 2 1/3 cups

Damn Tasty, Sure Simple Rib Sauce

When you're in a hurry, this sauce comes together quickly. It calls for ingredients commonly found in most kitchens.

3 tablespoons olive oil

4 cloves garlic, minced

1/3 cup firmly packed dark brown sugar

1/4 cup cider vinegar

2/3 cup chicken stock

1/4 cup tomato paste, or ketchup

3 tablespoons Dijon mustard

2 tablespoons soy sauce

1 tablespoon red pepper flakes

Heat the oil in a small, heavy saucepan over medium heat. Add garlic and sauté until transparent, 2 to 3 minutes. Do not allow the garlic to burn. Whisk in remaining ingredients, reduce heat to low; simmer 15 to 20 minutes, until the mixture thickens. Stir occasionally.

Yield: 1 1/2 cups

Savory Herb Barbecue Sauce

You could certainly use fresh herbs in this sauce. However, the results using dried herbs are quite good. If you let this sauce sit in the refrigerator overnight, the flavors will blend thoroughly.

1 tablespoon olive oil

1 medium red onion, finely chopped

2 cloves garlic, minced

1/2 teaspoon red pepper flakes

1/2 teaspoon basil

1/4 teaspoon oregano

1/4 teaspoon thyme

1/4 teaspoon cumin

1/4 teaspoon celery seeds

1/8 teaspoon cloves

1 teaspoon chile powder

1/2 teaspoon dry mustard

1 teaspoon salt

1/2 teaspoon coarsely cracked pepper

2 cups beef stock

1 can (6 ounces) tomato paste

1 cup tomato sauce

1/4 cup molasses

2 tablespoons firmly packed
   dark brown sugar

2 tablespoons cider vinegar

2 tablespoons Worcestershire sauce

1 tablespoon Kitchen Bouquet

1 tablespoon liquid smoke, optional

1 tablespoon prepared mustard

In a saucepan, combine the oil and onion over medium heat. Sauté until softened, about 5 minutes. Add garlic, red pepper flakes, basil, oregano, thyme, cumin, celery seeds, and cloves; cook 1 minute. Add chile powder, dry mustard, salt, and pepper and cook for 1 minute.

Pour in the stock and bring to a boil, stirring. Stir in the tomato paste, tomato sauce, molasses, and brown sugar. Add cider vinegar, Worcestershire sauce, Kitchen Bouquet, and liquid smoke and bring to a boil, stirring frequently. Reduce heat to low and simmer, stirring occasionally, until thick enough to coat a spoon and reduced to about 3 cups, about 1 hour. Watch carefully to prevent burning.

Yield: 3 cups

Bell's Barbecue in Syracuse, New York

Icuddahadda Sauce

This inspiration came from one of the wizards at a Madison Avenue ad agency. Inspired by the slogan, "Wow! I could've had a V-8!," I added some to a sauce and was pleased with the results. Two other unusual ingredients appear in this sauce, the under-appreciated prune juice and juniper berries. Substitute a few tablespoons of gin for the juniper berries if you can't find them.

1 tablespoon unsalted butter

1 medium onion, minced

1 clove garlic, minced

1 cup tomato sauce

1/2 cup cider vinegar

1/2 cup V-8 juice

1/4 cup prune juice

Grated peel from 1/4 lemon

Juice of 1/2 lemon

1 bay leaf

3 juniper berries, crushed

1/4 teaspoon cayenne

1 tablespoon firmly packed brown sugar

Melt butter in a saucepan over medium-low heat. Add the onion; cook 1 minute. Add the garlic; cook 2 minutes. Add remaining ingredients. Heat to a boil; reduce heat. Simmer, uncovered, until thickened, about 30 minutes. Remove bay leaf before using.

Yield: 3 cups

Fourth of July BBQ Sauce

What fourth of July would be complete without a barbecue? This basic, all-purpose sauce calls for these American pantry standards: ketchup, A-1, and Worcestershire.

1 tablespoon unsalted butter

1 onion, minced

3/4 cup ketchup

3 tablespoons Worcestershire sauce

2 tablespoons A-1 sauce

1 tablespoon cider vinegar

3 tablespoons firmly packed brown sugar

1/4 cup water

Tabasco, to taste

Melt butter in a saucepan over medium-low heat. Add the onion; cook 5 minutes. Be careful not to brown onions. Stir in remaining ingredients. Heat to boiling, then reduce heat. Simmer, uncovered, about 20 minutes.

Yield: 1 cup

Sesame and Ginger Marinade

This tasty, Asian-influenced marinade works great with jumbo shrimp or prawns. The marinade doesn't need to work too long; an hour will do for the shrimp. Reserve a portion of the marinade (which has not been used as a soak for the shrimp) as a dipping sauce.

4 large cloves garlic, crushed

2 teaspoons grated ginger

2 tablespoons sugar

2 tablespoons peanut oil

2 scallions, finely chopped

1/2 teaspoon red pepper flakes

2 tablespoons toasted sesame seeds

6 tablespoons soy sauce

2 tablespoons toasted sesame oil

1/4 cup rice wine vinegar

1/4 cup chopped cilantro

Combine all ingredients in a bowl.

Yield: 1 1/4 cups

Note: It's important not to use a marinade that has been used as a soak for any animal product as a dipping sauce. This sauce is also excellent on chicken.

Tandoori Marinade

This thinner rendition of tandoori sauce works nicely on chicken that is very slowly barbecued. Reserve some of the marinade to brush on the chicken to keep it moist.

Juice of 1/2 lemon

2 tablespoons salt

1/2 cup plain yogurt

2 cloves garlic, quartered

1 teaspoon minced ginger

1/2 teaspoon cumin seeds

1/2 teaspoon coriander

1/4 teaspoon turmeric

1/2 teaspoon cayenne

1/4 teaspoon freshly ground pepper

1/8 teaspoon cinnamon

1/8 teaspoon cloves

Mix ingredients together in a bowl. Let stand at room temperature for about 30 minutes to let the flavors blend.

Yield: 3/4 cup

Lina's Chinese Barbecue Sauce for Pork

Here is a sauce for a slightly different barbecued pork, more lean and garlicky than traditional Chinese char siu. It makes an impressive sight as it roasts to a crusty brown color.

1/2 cup ketchup
1/4 cup hoisin sauce
2 tablespoons brandy
2 teaspoons oyster sauce
1/2 cup sugar
2 tablespoons minced garlic
1 teaspoon salt

Combine all the ingredients. Mix well. Allow to stand 15 minutes to blend the flavors.

Yield: 1 cup

Thyme-Mustard Sauce

This simple mix is actually very elegant. Use it as a finishing sauce with chicken or pork tenderloin.

3/4 cup light or heavy cream
1/4 cup Dijon mustard
3 tablespoons thyme leaves
1/8 teaspoon white pepper

Combine all ingredients in a small bowl. Just before serving, warm the mixture in a microwave until it simmers, or place it in the top of a double boiler and bring to a low boil.

Yield: 1 cup

Mint-Rosemary Sauce

The mint adds a cool, slightly sweet flavor to this sauce. You might want to try it on salmon.

1/2 cup dry red wine
1/4 cup apple cider
1/4 cup minced mint
2 tablespoons fresh rosemary leaves, or 1 tablespoon dried
2 tablespoons white wine vinegar
2 tablespoons confectioners sugar
Salt and pepper to taste

Combine all ingredients in a saucepan and bring to a simmer over medium heat. Cook 3 to 4 minutes, stirring occasionally. Refrigerate sauce 40 minutes or longer before using.

Yield: 1 cup

SAUCEMASTER TIP

"One way to grate fresh ginger easily is to freeze it first. By doing this, it's less pulpy and doesn't clog the grater up. Once you try this method, you'll never grate unfrozen ginger again!"
—Ed Hohberg, Oregon meat burner

Cattle Drive Barbecue Sauce

A surprisingly large number of sauce recipes call for coffee as a key ingredient. It also seems to be the secret ingredient in a number of chili recipes. I can only guess at the origin. Probably some cowpoke dumped his coffee into the chuck wagon cook's stew pot in hopes of "perking up" the taste.

1 large onion, coarsely chopped

1/2 cup brewed coffee, the blacker the better

1/2 cup Worcestershire sauce

1/4 cup cider vinegar

2 tablespoons chile powder

1/2 cup ketchup

1/4 cup firmly packed dark brown sugar

1/4 cup chopped canned green chiles

1 tablespoon chopped garlic

1 tablespoon salt

In a saucepan, simmer all the ingredients, stirring occasionally, for 25 minutes. Let the mixture cool. In a blender, purée sauce in batches until smooth.

Yield: 2 cups

State Fair Barbecue Sauce

I don't recall many childhood summers that I missed the State Fair. It signaled the end of summer and impending school days. Fortunately, the fair also signaled chow time, corn on the cob, cotton candy, watermelon—and of course barbecue. Things were much simpler then.

1 medium onion, minced

1 bunch scallions, white portions only, minced

1/2 green bell pepper, minced

5 cloves garlic, minced

1/4 cup chicken broth

2 cups ketchup

1/4 cup Worcestershire sauce

1/4 cup cider vinegar

1/2 cup dark beer

2 tablespoons mustard

3 tablespoons firmly packed dark brown sugar

1 teaspoon chile powder

1 teaspoon cumin

Sauté the onion, scallions, pepper, and garlic in the broth. Be careful not to brown them. Remove to a large bowl. Add the remaining ingredients and blend thoroughly. Let stand, covered, 1 or more hours, until ready to use.

Yield: 3 1/4 cups

Nuts-About-You Barbecue Sauce

This two-part recipe calls for a spice blend which is then mixed into a sauce. Use the resulting sauce as a finishing baste or dipping sauce. The bacon and pecans work surprisingly well together. Walnuts can be substituted for the pecans.

Seasoning mix:

1 teaspoon pepper

1/2 teaspoon salt

1/2 teaspoon onion powder

1/2 teaspoon garlic powder

1/8 teaspoon white pepper

1/8 teaspoon cayenne, to taste

Sauce:

1/4 pound bacon, minced

3/4 cup chopped onions

2 cups chicken or beef broth

1 cup bottled chili sauce or ketchup

1/2 cup honey

1/2 cup dry-roasted, unsalted pecans, coarsely chopped

2 tablespoons orange juice

1 tablespoon lemon juice

Chopped rind from 1/4 orange

Chopped rind from 1/4 lemon

1 teaspoon minced garlic

1 teaspoon Tabasco

2 tablespoons unsalted butter

Combine seasoning mix ingredients in a small bowl and set aside. In a saucepan, fry bacon over high heat until crisp. Stir in onions, cover pan, and continue cooking until onions are dark brown but not burned, 8 to 10 minutes. Stir the mixture occasionally. Add seasoning mix and cook about 1 minute. Add remaining ingredients except butter, stirring well. Reduce heat to low; continue cooking about 10 minutes, stirring frequently. Remove the orange and lemon rinds. Continue cooking and stirring, about 15 minutes. Add butter and stir until melted. Remove from heat. Let cool about 30 minutes; pour into a food processor or blender and process until the pecans and bacon are finely chopped, about 10 to 20 seconds.

Yield: 5 1/2 cups

It's the Law!

Leave it to the legislators of South Carolina to show the world they're serious about barbecue! In 1986, that state's elected officials passed a "Truth in Barbecue Law." Barbecue restaurants must purchase a sticker, telling patrons if they cook with wood or by another means. The sticker also identifies restaurants that cook whole hogs and those that do not.

Loozieanna Cookin' Sauce

While I can't say that I've tried too much Louisiana barbecue, this one caught my fancy. Gumbo file is a spice blend that you will find in most grocery stores.

1 cup ketchup
1/2 cup cider vinegar
1/2 cup water
1/2 cup firmly packed brown sugar
3 tablespoons Worcestershire sauce
2 tablespoons cracked pepper
1 tablespoon salt
1 tablespoon lemon juice
1 tablespoon dry mustard
1 tablespoon gumbo file
3 tablespoons hot pepper sauce, to taste
2 tablespoons juice from 1 jar jalapeños
1 tablespoons red pepper flakes
1/2 teaspoon cayenne

Mix all ingredients and simmer 20 minutes. I find it best to let a sauce like this stand for 15 to 20 minutes, to let the ingredients blend into a harmonious whole.

Yield: 2 1/2 cups

Jack Daniels Barbecue Glaze

The good folks at the Jack Daniels distillery have certainly made their mark on the barbecue world. Several excellent recipes call for Jack Daniels whiskey. I like this one.

1 cup Jack Daniels
1/2 cup firmly packed dark brown sugar
1 cup ketchup
1 teaspoon Worcestershire sauce
1/4 cup cider vinegar
1 tablespoon lemon juice
3 cloves garlic, minced
1/2 teaspoon dry mustard
Salt and pepper to taste

Combine all ingredients; mix well.

Yield: 2 1/2 cups

The Central Texan Barbecue in Castroville, California

Coffee Barbecue Sauce

1 cup ketchup

2/3 cup strong coffee

1/2 cup firmly packed brown sugar

1/4 cup cider vinegar

1 teaspoon garlic powder

3 tablespoons Worcestershire sauce

2 tablespoons hot pepper sauce

1/2 teaspoon dried Italian seasoning

In a bowl, mix all ingredients. No cooking required!

Yield: 2 1/2 cups

Curried Tomato Sauce

Be careful with curry powder as it can be a dominating spice. The balance of flavors is very good in this recipe.

3 tablespoons curry powder

1 teaspoon cumin

2 tablespoons olive oil

1/2 cup tomato sauce

2 tablespoons fresh lemon juice

1 teaspoon sugar

In a saucepan, fry curry powder, cumin, and oil over moderate heat until mixture begins to sizzle. Cook mixture, stirring, 1 minute more, then add remaining ingredients. Cook sauce, stirring, until smooth, about 10 minutes.

Yield: 3/4 cup

Headhunter's Satay

Culinary explorer and adventurer Richard Sterling came out of the jungle alive with his head still on his shoulders and this recipe for satay in his pocket. This recipe works great on pork in particular.

1 strip lemon peel

1 red onion, chopped

1 tablespoon soy sauce

2 tablespoons vegetable oil

1 teaspoon coriander seeds

1 tablespoon chopped cilantro stalks

1 teaspoon cumin

1 teaspoon turmeric

1/4 teaspoon cinnamon

1 teaspoon sugar

1 teaspoon salt

2 tablespoons unsalted peanuts, finely chopped

1 fresh chile, such as serrano, chopped

2 cloves garlic

Place all ingredients in food processor. Pulse lightly to chop and mix ingredients. Allow to stand for a bit to enhance the flavors. If you don't want so much heat, take the seeds out of the chile before you process it.

Yield: 1 cup

Colonel Mustard in the Library Sauce

I don't have a clue where I came up with this title or this sauce for that matter. But I did and it's good.

1/4 cup olive oil

2 cloves garlic, pressed

1 teaspoon salt

1/3 cup firmly packed brown sugar

1/3 cup apple cider vinegar

1/4 cup Dijon mustard

1/4 cup grainy mustard

2 tablespoons honey

2 teaspoons dried thyme

2 teaspoons dried tarragon

Whisk all ingredients together. The sauce needs no cooking. I use it as a finishing baste for chicken.

Yield: 1 1/2 cups

The Father of American Mustard

The honor belongs to New Jersey resident and entrepreneur Francis French, who introduced the U.S. to a special blend of the familiar yellow condiment that carries his name.

Spicy Peanut Sauce

This works best as a finishing baste and for dipping. It also makes a great sauce for noodles.

2 tablespoons minced garlic

1 small knob ginger, peeled and grated

1/4 cup chopped cilantro

1/2 cup soy sauce

1/4 cup sugar

1 cup crunchy peanut butter

2 tablespoons toasted sesame oil

1/2 cup chicken broth

2 tablespoons hot chile oil, or a bit of chile powder with olive oil

Combine all the ingredients except broth and chile oil in a food processor and blend. Slowly add chicken broth and chile oil and blend well. In a saucepan, heat the mixture to a low boil, then remove from heat. Allow to cool.

Yield: 2 cups

Flame-thrower Sauces

*P*ut the fire department on standby! These sauces are inspired by the very fires of hell. Flame-thrower sauces aren't for the meek and mild. Unlike their sweet or savory cousins, these sauces are meant to be taken seriously. Many of these recipes contain the habanero pepper, sometimes called the scotch bonnet, 30 to 100 times more intense in heat than the mild-mannered jalapeño.

One very important precaution when dealing with hot peppers is that you must never handle the peppers and then touch your eyes or other sensitive body parts.

Overleaf: Hole in the Wall Barbecue in Eugene, Oregon; Paul Kirk (the Baron of Barbecue).

Hot Orange-Chile Glaze

Combinations of citrus and chile pepper can work quite well together. Try different types of peppers and citrus—you'll find some appealing combinations. This glaze can transform duck into a very special dish.

1 tablespoon vegetable oil

1 medium yellow onion, minced

1 tablespoon minced garlic

3 serrano chiles, diced small

1 tablespoon coriander seed

2 tablespoons chile powder

1 tablespoon cumin

Salt and freshly cracked pepper, to taste

1/2 cup orange juice

2 tablespoons molasses

1/2 cup white vinegar

1/2 cup chicken broth

2 tablespoons cornstarch

4 tablespoons cold water

In a heavy-bottomed saucepan, heat oil until hot but not smoking. Sauté onion in oil over medium heat until clear, 5 to 7 minutes. Add garlic and serranos, and cook an additional 2 minutes. Add remaining ingredients, except cornstarch and water, and bring mixture to a boil. Simmer 20 minutes, stirring occasionally.

In a small bowl, mix cornstarch and water together thoroughly. Slowly stir mixture into the simmering glaze until thickened; remove from heat.

Yield: 2 cups

Elvira-Inspired Barbecue Sauce

The Queen of the Night gave me the inspiration for this sauce. Like her, this sauce is hot and spicy. For an inspired hot pepper sauce, try Red Devil, Mean Devil Woman, or Scorned Woman.

8 ounces hot pepper sauce

1 tablespoon red pepper flakes

1 small red onion, chopped

1 cup tomato purée

3/4 cup water

3/4 cup sugar

Juice of 1 lemon

Combine all ingredients in a heavy pot and heat. Do not allow sauce to boil or it will turn dark and become thin. Let cool to room temperature before using.

Yield: 3 cups

A Spicy Top Five

According to the latest available information from the American Spice Trade Association, the five most widely used spices in the nation are mustard (seeds, dry, powder), black pepper, cayenne, cumin, and cinnamon.

Wildman Willie's Quein' Sauce

I used to play hoops with a guy called Wildman Willie. He couldn't shoot straight, but (I found out later) he sure could barbecue.

2 tablespoons Hungarian hot paprika

2 tablespoons onion granules

1 teaspoon oregano

1 tablespoon cumin

1 teaspoon pepper

2 teaspoons garlic granules

1 teaspoon crushed red pepper flakes

1 teaspoon salt

2 teaspoons cayenne

1 teaspoon coriander

1/8 teaspoon ground celery seed

1/8 teaspoon nutmeg

2 dashes allspice

1/4 cup flat Coca-Cola

1 1/2 cups water

1 can (6 ounces) tomato paste

1 ounce bittersweet chocolate bits

1/2 small can (3 ounces) frozen orange juice concentrate

1 cup cider vinegar

1/4 cup molasses

2 teaspoons soy sauce

1 teaspoon Worcestershire sauce

1/8 cup vegetable oil

1/8 cup red wine

1/4 cup coffee

1 tablespoon prepared horseradish

In a small bowl, combine all the dry spices with the cola to make a paste. In a large, heavy enamel or stainless steel pot, bring water to a boil, then whisk in the paste. Add the rest of the ingredients to the pot, stirring continuously, until it boils again. Reduce heat immediately and let simmer 15 minutes; remove from burner and let cool. Pour sauce into plastic jugs, cover, and store in a cool place.

Yield: 5 cups

Fiery Lime-Cilantro Sauce

This is an old favorite of mine, a warm tropical type of sauce. You can brush it on pork or chicken or use it as a finishing sauce.

1/2 cup fresh cilantro leaves

1/2 teaspoon grated lime peel

1/2 teaspoon salt

1/3 teaspoon cayenne

1 tablespoon Tabasco

1/2 cup butter, softened

Combine cilantro, lime zest, salt, cayenne, and Tabasco in a food processor. Pulse ingredients several times until cilantro and lime peel are finely chopped. Add butter and mix in food processor for about 30 seconds.

Yield: 1 1/4 cups

Heat Up Yer Honey

If you'd like to heat up your honey, try this Sandi Bjorkman trick: Add one or two habanero or chile peppers to your jar of honey. Allow the peppers to soak in the sweet liquid for two weeks, then remove them. You'll find that the heat-producing capsicum has been absorbed by the honey, heating the honey up by a considerable degree. Delicious!

Kim's Hot Wing Sauce

My friend Kim Wallis must have a heat-resistant tongue—or one that's heat-tempered. Here's one of his down-home hot recipes for use on chicken wings.

1 cup hot pepper sauce

1/2 cup honey

1/2 cup frozen orange juice concentrate, slightly thawed

1 tablespoon garlic granules

1 tablespoon finely minced cilantro leaves

1 teaspoon freshly ground pepper

1 teaspoon ground pascilla chile

1 teaspoon onion granules

Blend all ingredients together in a food processor until smooth. Pour over wings in a shallow bowl and marinate for 30 minutes prior to cooking. Use remainder as a baste while grilling.

Yield: 2 1/3 cups

Dakota Kid's Buffalo Breath Garlic-Jalapeño Paste

In just two short years, Harold Froescher, aka The Dakota Kid, has racked up an impressive number of blue ribbons and Grand Championship wins along the Northwest barbecue contest circuit. This mixture goes well with beef and pork and is also a heck of a chip dip. A little goes a long way, so the paste may be a little strong for uninitiated palates. Adjust the garlic and peppers downward if you like, but note they are somewhat tamed by the roasting process.

4 heads garlic
4 jalapeños, peeled and seeded
1/4 cup olive oil

Roast the garlic heads and jalapeños in a 400° oven for 30 minutes. Squeeze the garlic pulp out of the cloves. Put all the ingredients in a food processor and process until the mixture becomes a paste. You may add more oil, a tablespoon at a time, to thin the paste to the desired consistency.

Yield: 1/2 to 1/3 cup

Thanks to Harold Froescher of West Linn, Oregon

Hot Orange Spice Barbecue Sauce

You can easily change the complexity and heat level of any sauce recipe with the addition of any hot chile. With a little experimentation, I found a way to jazz up a traditional Georgia barbecue sauce recipe and add a little summertime heat to it. You can also increase or decrease the amount of cayenne to the level of heat you or your guests can stand. The sauce can be thickened if you like with cornstarch and used as a glaze on white fish or pork.

1/2 cup dry red wine
1/2 cup orange marmalade
1/2 cup ketchup
1/8 cup soy sauce
1/4 cup olive oil
1/8 cup Worcestershire sauce
1 small onion, chopped
1 teaspoon chile powder
1 teaspoon pepper
1/2 teaspoon dry mustard
1/2 teaspoon cayenne

Combine all ingredients in a saucepan. Bring mixture to boil and allow to simmer with the lid on for 1 hour. Let mixture cool; place in food processor and blend until smooth.

Yield: 2 cups

Buzzin' Bee Honey-Q-Sauce

Honey is an ideal barbecue sauce ingredient as it adds sweetness but doesn't overwhelm the other ingredients. It mixes well with other flavors and, best of all, sticks to the food! This mixture does snap back at you with the bite of 3 different peppers. Cocoa powder is the mysterious ingredient in this mix.

1 cup ketchup

1 can (6 ounces) tomato paste

1 1/2 cups light honey

1 1/2 teaspoons olive oil

2 teaspoons Tabasco

1 teaspoon cayenne

1 fresh habanero pepper, seeded and minced

1 tablespoon Worcestershire sauce

1 tablespoon cocoa powder

1 teaspoon lemon juice

1/2 tablespoon soy sauce

1/2 teaspoon pepper

1 1/2 tablespoons curry powder

1 tablespoon paprika

2 cloves garlic, put through a press

In a saucepan, stir everything together and simmer 20 to 30 minutes. Please do not boil.

Yield: 3 cups

Miami Spice Seafood Barbecue Sauce

Sonny Crockett and his Miami Vice gator were the inspiration for this sauce, which works best on seafood. Try it on a firm fish like swordfish or halibut. Habanero peppers and scotch bonnets are basically the same.

3 cloves garlic, chopped

2 medium onions, diced

3 scotch bonnet peppers, seeded, deveined, and minced

1 bay leaf

1/4 cup peanut oil

1 cup chopped pear tomatoes

1 bottle (12 ounces) amber beer

1 cup chicken stock

1 tablespoon cumin

1 cup firmly packed brown sugar

3 tablespoons Worcestershire sauce

1 1/2 tablespoons cornstarch

1/4 cup cold water

Sauté garlic, onions, peppers, and bay leaf in oil over high heat in a large, heavy saucepan until they start to caramelize. Add tomatoes, beer, and stock, then reduce heat to medium-high. Continue cooking until the mixture is reduced by 1/2, then add cumin, sugar, and Worcestershire. Combine cornstarch with water. Add cornstarch mix to sauce and boil 5 minutes, stirring well. Serve at room temperature as a finish to grilled seafood or as a sauce topping.

Yield: 3 cups

Harissa

Moroccan Spiced Red Chile Paste

This paste can be extremely hot depending on the chile peppers. Remember you can always add heat to a dish, so be cautious with the peppers. Use the paste as a rub before or after barbecuing your meat.

1/2 to 1 cup small dried red chiles

Boiling water to cover chiles

1 tablespoon cumin

2 teaspoons curry powder

1/2 teaspoon salt

2 tablespoons olive oil

Place chiles in a heatproof bowl and cover with boiling water. Let stand 30 minutes to 1 hour. Drain, reserving some of the soaking water.

Place chiles in blender or food processor with 1/4 cup soaking water. Purée until smooth, scraping down the sides of the container a few times. Add spices, salt, and olive oil and blend well.

Yield: 1 cup

SAUCEMASTER TIP

Cumin is a spice with a strong, musty aroma, somewhat like caraway. Like coriander, cumin loses its aromatic oils soon after grinding. For best results purchase whole cumin seed and grind just prior to use.

Colorado Chile Que Sauce

This recipe calls for an unusual product: smoked habanero powder. This can be found at any of the hot sauce shops that are popping up all over the country. If you can't find it, add more chile powder than the 2 tablespoons called for here. You will still have a fine sauce.

2 tablespoons unsalted butter

1 medium onion, minced

1 clove garlic, minced

1 can (12 ounces) dark beer

1/2 cup tomato juice

1/4 cup Worcestershire sauce

1/4 cup firmly packed brown sugar

Juice of 1/2 lemon

1 tablespoon Hungarian sweet paprika

2 tablespoons Dijon mustard

2 tablespoons chile powder

1 teaspoon crushed red pepper flakes

1 teaspoon smoked habanero powder

Pinch of marjoram

Pinch of thyme

1/2 teaspoon salt

1/4 teaspoon freshly ground pepper

1 tablespoon tomato paste

Melt butter in a medium saucepan over medium-low heat. Add the onion; cook 1 minute. Add garlic, cook 4 minutes. Stir in remaining ingredients. Heat to boiling; reduce heat and simmer, uncovered, 30 minutes.

Yield: 1 1/2 cups

Berberé
Arabic Chile and Spice Paste

In an old Middle Eastern travel journal, I came across a recipe that called for camel meat with a paste similar to this recipe. I've adjusted the recipe and omitted the camel. Try this with something less exotic, but still interesting, like goat or venison.

2 cups small dried red chiles

Boiling water to cover chiles

2 teaspoons cumin

1 onion, minced

2 cloves garlic, minced

1 tablespoon ginger

1 teaspoon turmeric

1 teaspoon freshly ground pepper

1 teaspoon salt

Seeds from 4 cardamom pods

Remove stems (and seeds as well, if you want to tame the fire) from the chiles. Cover chiles with boiling water and let stand until softened, 30 minutes or so. Toast cumin in a dry heavy skillet until color darkens and aroma becomes more fragrant. Drain chiles, reserving a bit of the liquid. Purée chiles with onion, garlic, seasonings, and a tiny bit of the soaking water.

Yield: 2 cups

Variations of Berberé from other African nations:

Shata (Sudan)

Combine 3 tablespoons Berberé with 1 extra clove garlic, minced, and 1 cup lemon juice.

Yield: 1 1/3 cups

Sakay (Malagasy Republic)

Combine 3 tablespoons Berberé with 1 clove garlic, minced, 1 teaspoon ginger, and 1 tablespoon oil.

Yield: 5 tablespoons

Hickory Pit Bar-B-Q in Kansas City, Missouri

Who Do Voodoo Sauce

This works well with poultry and seafood.

1 tablespoon toasted sesame oil

2 red bell peppers, seeded and chopped

1 onion, peeled and chopped

2 cloves garlic, minced

1 ancho chile, seeded and chopped

1 serrano chile, chopped

1 habanero pepper, seeded and chopped

1 ripe tomato, chopped

1 papaya, peeled, seeded, and chopped

1 tablespoon firmly packed brown sugar

1 tablespoon grated ginger

3 tablespoons hot pepper sauce

1/2 cup sweet rice wine vinegar

1/2 cup chicken broth

1/2 cup orange juice

1 teaspoon fish sauce

1 teaspoon soy sauce

Salt, to taste

Fresh lime juice, to taste

Heat oil in large saucepan over medium heat. Add red peppers, onions, garlic, and all chiles. Sauté 3 to 4 minutes, until onions are transparent. Add tomatoes, papaya, brown sugar, ginger, hot pepper sauce, vinegar, chicken broth, and orange juice, and bring to a boil. Turn heat down and simmer mixture 30 minutes. Pour in a blender and process until smooth. Strain. Add fish sauce and soy sauce; season with salt and lime juice.

Yield: 2 1/2 cups

Dominican Barbecue Sauce

Put on some Calypso music, a straw hat, and your flip-flops, break out the rum punch, and head down to the islands with this Caribbean inspiration.

1/4 cup mango nectar, or puréed fresh mango*

1/4 cup tamarind nectar, or puréed fresh tamarind*

1/4 cup ketchup

2 tablespoons white vinegar

2 tablespoons firmly packed dark brown sugar

1 tablespoon butter

1 tablespoon lime or lemon juice

1/2 teaspoon salt

1 medium onion, finely grated

1 clove garlic, minced

1/2 cup water

Combine all the ingredients in a saucepan over medium heat, stirring well. Bring to a boil, reduce heat, and simmer 10 minutes, stirring frequently.

Yield: 1 1/2 cups

*Mango and tamarind nectar are widely available in supermarkets under the Goya and Libby labels.

Jerk Marinade

This marinade, while not as fiery as a jerk rub, is still quite hot. It lends itself to lighter meats and seafood and does not require long marinating times: 2 to 3 hours for chicken, less than an hour for seafood will yield satisfying results. This marinade is good for chicken, beef, or pork.

1 onion, minced

2 habanero peppers, seeded, deveined, and minced

1/2 cup minced scallions

2 teaspoons thyme leaves

1 teaspoon salt

2 teaspoons sugar

1 teaspoon allspice

1/2 teaspoon nutmeg

1/2 teaspoon cinnamon

1 teaspoon pepper

3 tablespoons soy sauce

1 tablespoon vegetable oil

1 tablespoon white vinegar

Mix together all the ingredients. A food processor fitted with a steel blade is ideal for chopping and combining the ingredients.

Yield: 1 1/2 cups

5-4-3-2-1, Blast-Off!

Using the Scoville Heat Unit Scale as our guide, here's a list of hot peppers from the chief conflagration flame-thrower to the small burn variety:

1. Habanero pepper (150,000–300,000)
2. Japanese kumataka (125,000–150,000)
3. Birdseye (India) (100,000–125,000)
4. Cayenne pepper (100,000–105,000)
5. Mexican tabiche (90,000–100,000)

—From Peppers: A Story of Hot Pursuits by Amal Naj

Mole Verde

Try this variation of the classic mole that calls for chile and chocolate. I thank Caryl Hill of Rosa's Rotisseria in Santa Cruz, California, for this recipe. It is best used as a baste for barbecued chicken.

1 tablespoon olive oil

2 medium onions, diced

4 serrano chiles, seeded and membranes removed, minced

2 cloves garlic, minced

2 cups fresh tomatillos, peeled and diced

1/2 tablespoon cumin

1/2 tablespoon coriander

2 cups chicken broth

2 corn tortilla chips, unsalted, crumbled

1/2 cup pumpkin seeds, toasted

1/2 cup diced papaya

1 cup chopped cilantro leaves

1/2 cup chopped fresh spinach leaves

Salt, to taste

Fresh lime juice, to taste

Heat oil in a large saucepan over medium heat. Add onions and sauté 5 minutes, until golden. Add serranos, garlic, tomatillos, and spices, and sauté for about 6 minutes, until mixture is fairly dry and vegetables begin to brown slightly.

Add chicken stock, tortilla chips, pumpkin seeds, and papaya. Bring to a boil. Lower heat and simmer 15 minutes. Pour into a blender. Add cilantro, spinach, salt, and lime juice, and purée until smooth.

Yield: 3 cups

Record Heatwave

The hottest commercially grown pepper ever measured on the Scoville Heat Unit (SHU) Scale was a red savina habanero pepper, grown by GNS Spices. The monster hot pepper measured 577,000 Scoville Units. By comparison, the average commercially grown habanero pepper ranges between 150,000 and 350,000 SHUs.

Secret Recipes of the Pitmasters

*I*f you think Fort Knox does a good job guarding America's gold supply, try wheedling a secret sauce recipe from a champion barbecuer! However, by hook, crook, and a lot of begging, I've been fortunate to convince some of the nation's premier barbecuers to provide us with their favorite recipes. They aren't saying whether any of these sauces is "the one." They only smile and say, "I'll never tell!"

Whenever possible, visit local or regional cookoffs and watch the teams at work. You'd be surprised how much you can learn just by observing them. If you're real nice, some pro might even share a taste of their fabulous "que." That is, after they've turned in their entries for judging.

Overleaf: Judges at the 1995 Oregon Open, Springfield Oregon; Steve "Roscoe" Ross, former National Barbecue Association president.

Wilber's South Carolina Chicken Sauce

Wilber King oversees three restaurants in Kinston, North Carolina, that his father started in 1946. Wilber believes in doing things in a BIG way, having initiated one of the first overnight barbecue delivery services in the country, The Carolina Oink Express (1-800-332-OINK). Here's his recipe for barbecuing up a mess of chicken, just right for those summertime family reunions.

1 quart apple cider vinegar

8 ounces tomato paste

1/4 cup peanut oil

1/8 cup steak sauce (A-1 brand sauce preferred)

1/8 cup Worcestershire sauce

1/8 cup hot pepper sauce

1/4 cup sugar

1/4 cup salt

Pour all ingredients into large saucepan. Simmer the mixture for five minutes. Let cool. Marinate the chicken overnight. Remove some of the sauce for basting the chicken while you are barbecuing it.

Yield: 6 cups

From Wilber King of Kinston, North Carolina

Paul Kirk's Grilled Chicken Sauce

This recipe makes enough sauce for two chickens, each split in half.

1/4 cup vegetable oil

1/4 cup dry white wine

1/4 cup chicken broth

2 tablespoons lemon juice

2 tablespoons apple jelly

1 teaspoon salt

1 teaspoon snipped parsley

1/2 teaspoon prepared mustard

1/2 teaspoon Worcestershire sauce

1/4 teaspoon celery seed

1/4 teaspoon rosemary

1/4 teaspoon pepper

Combine all ingredients in a saucepan. Beat out jelly lumps with a wire whisk. Brush mixture over the chickens. Place the chickens on the grill, bone-side down over low heat. Baste frequently while cooking, approximately 1 hour, or until chicken is tender and the skin is crisp.

Yield: 1 cup

From Paul Kirk, Ph.B., of Shawnee Mission, Kansas

The Baron's Sweet & Spicy Barbecue Sauce

Paul Kirk is one of the undisputed practitioners of barbecue. A founding member of the Kansas City Barbecue Society, he's won so many contests that he's been named "Baron of Barbecue." Paul is one of the few C.W.C.s, (Certified Working Chefs) to actively promote barbecue. That Ph.B. by his name is an official doctorate degree, conferred upon him by the Kansas City Barbecue Society. Here's one of his favorite sauce recipes:

Dry ingredients

1/4 cup firmly packed brown sugar

3/4 teaspoon chili powder

1/4 tablespoon pepper

1/4 tablespoon salt

1/4 tablespoon garlic granules

1/2 teaspoon onion granules

1/4 teaspoon allspice

1/4 teaspoon cayenne

1/8 teaspoon cloves

1/8 teaspoon mace

1/8 teaspoon bay leaf

Liquid ingredients

1/4 cup molasses

1/4 cup clover honey

1/3 cup white vinegar

2 tablespoons Worcestershire sauce

1/2 teaspoon liquid smoke

1 teaspoon jalapeño pepper juice

1/2 cup ketchup

1 4-ounce can tomato paste

1/2 cup water

Put the dry ingredients in a large saucepan. Add all of the liquid ingredients, except ketchup, tomato paste and water. Over medium heat, stir all ingredients until they dissolve. Blend in ketchup, tomato paste, and water and bring mixture to a boil. Reduce heat and simmer for thirty minutes. Use this sauce at room temperature.

Yield: about 3 1/2 cups

From Paul Kirk, Ph.B., of Shawnee Mission, Kansas

Now the whole deal about barbecue cooking is the history. If you want to understand the food, you have to know something about the past.

—Sam Higgins, famous Texan barbecuer

Remus's Kansas City Classic Sauce

Remus is one of those great barbecue characters you get to meet along the trail. Back in 1988 on his patio, he started what has become the world's largest commercial barbecue sauce contest, now held each October in conjunction with the KCBS American Royal Invitational Cookoff. Remus is barbecue's ultimate saucemeister. Here's his recipe for a classic Kansas City barbecue sauce:

1/4 teaspoon allspice

1/4 teaspoon cinnamon

1/4 teaspoon mace

1/4 teaspoon pepper

1/2 teaspoon curry powder, oriental preferred

1/2 teaspoon chili powder

1/2 teaspoon paprika

1/4 cup white vinegar

1/2 teaspoon hot pepper sauce

1 cup ketchup

1/3 cup dark molasses

Place all of the dry ingredients into a bowl. Add vinegar and stir. Add remaining ingredients and stir until mixture is thoroughly blended. This sauce may be served room temperature or heated.

Yield: 2 cups

From Remus Powers, Ph.B., Originator of the Diddy-Wa-Diddy Sauce Contest

Diddy-Wa-Diddy Mop and Basting Sauce

"This is a simple flavor enhancer" Remus tells me. "It's thin enough to read today's headlines through . . . but not so thin that a politician can." That Remus, political commentator and barbecuing star . . . Remus assures me that this authentic sauce can be used as a mop during cooking and as a dip after your meat has been taken off the grill.

1/4 teaspoon pepper

1/4 teaspoon salt

1/2 teaspoon hot pepper sauce

1/4 cup white vinegar

1 cup white grape juice

Combine all ingredients in a jar. Tighten lid and shake until blended. This sauce may be served at room temperature or heated.

Yield: 1 1/2 cups

From Remus Powers, Ph.B.

Dan Green's Sauce for Pork

It's mostly Dan Green's fault that I allowed my passion for barbecue to hit high gear. Back in the late '80s, I used to sell Dan radio advertising. During the course of our business deals, we discovered each other's passion for great barbecue. We'd phone each other up on Mondays and brag about how good our backyard barbecue was. Here's a recipe Dan developed for pork butt (Boston butt), a category we're still trying to win ribbons in. But the sauce is good whether you win or not!

3 cups ketchup

1/4 cup sugar

1/2 cup tarragon vinegar

1 medium onion, minced

2 tablespoons Worcestershire sauce

2 tablespoons chili powder

1 tablespoon cayenne

1 tablespoon garlic salt

Combine all ingredients in a saucepan and cook over medium heat for 10 minutes. Stir frequently. Allow to cool down to room temperature. Brush the mixture on the pork during the final phase of cooking; if using indirect heat, you may use it as a mop.

Yield: 3 3/4 cups

From Dan Green of Salem, Oregon

Beaver Castor's All-Purpose Rub

Bob Lyon is the Pacific Northwest's "Mr. Barbecue." He is responsible for founding the Pacific Northwest Barbecue Association and is the head cook of the Beaver Castor's cooking team, which in 1993 took Reserve Champion honors at the prestigious American Royal and Jack Daniels's Invitational cookoffs. Bob says this rub can be used on any type of meat with great success. Take it from me, this team knows how to cook great-tasting barbecue. They've won contests every year since 1988.

1/2 cup sugar

1/8 cup garlic salt

1/8 cup onion salt

1/8 cup celery salt

1/8 cup seasoned salt

1/4 cup pepper

1/4 cup paprika

1/4 cup chile seasoning

1 teaspoon dry mustard

1/4 teaspoon oregano or cumin

1/4 teaspoon ginger

1/4 teaspoon cloves

Combine ingredients in a bowl or jar with a screw-on lid. Shake until thoroughly blended.

Yield: 2 cups

From Bob Lyon, Ph.B., Head Cook, of Bellevue, Washington

Bob Lyon's Cajun Barbecue Sauce

This tangy recipe from bayou country goes best with some zydeco music playing in the background.

1/4 cup flat beer

1 teaspoon onion powder

1 teaspoon garlic powder

1 teaspoon pepper

1/2 teaspoon white pepper

1/2 teaspoon cayenne

1/2 teaspoon salt

1/2 pound bacon, chopped

1 medium yellow onion, chopped

2 cups beef stock

1-1/2 cups chile sauce

1/4 cup orange juice

1 cup honey

2 tablespoons lemon juice

1 tablespoon Tabasco

1/2 cup finely chopped pecans

4 cloves minced garlic

1/4 cup butter

In a large stockpot, combine the beer and spices. Set aside. Fry bacon and onion until bacon is crisp and onion is golden. Drain off bacon fat. Add bacon bits and onion to stockpot. Add remaining ingredients except the butter. Simmer for 2 hours over medium heat. Keep the pot covered. Add the butter after 2 hours, then allow mixture to cool. Place the sauce in batches in a blender or food processor and blend until smooth. Refrigerate the sauce overnight before using.

Yield: 4 cups

From Bob Lyon, Ph.B., of Bellevue, Washington

The Beaver Castors at the 1995 American Royal in Kansas City

Ron's Mandarin-Hickory Chipotle Barbecue Sauce

The chipotle pepper is enjoying wide popularity with many chefs these days. Chef Ron Romo from the Monterey Bay area recommends this smoky-tangy sauce for use with seafood or chicken.

1/4 cup minced onion

1/4 cup minced garlic

2 tablespoons olive oil

4 ounces sake

16 ounces tomato sauce

4 ounces canned chipotles

4 ounces chile colorado sauce
  (available in most Hispanic markets)

3 tablespoons soy sauce

1 tablespoon Worcestershire sauce

4 tablespoons maple syrup

4 ounces canned mandarin oranges, puréed

1 1/2 tablespoons hickory seasoning
  liquid (similar to Liquid Smoke)

1 tablespoon sweet rice wine vinegar

In a small saucepan over low heat, heat the olive oil, then add onion, garlic, and sake. Reduce mixture over medium heat for 5 minutes. Let cool. In a blender, place the sautéed onions, garlic, and sake with tomato sauce, chipotles, and chile colorado sauce; blend thoroughly. Pour mixture into saucepan and add all remaining ingredients except vinegar. Slowly simmer for 15 minutes, add the vinegar, and cook for 5 minutes more. Allow to cool.

Yield: 2 1/2 cups

From Ron Romo of Monterey, California

The Campbell Family's Texas Sop

Felton Campbell is a big bear of a man, as gentle as he is tall. Sitting at a neatly set table in his family-owned restaurant, he reminisces about growing up in the Texas hill country, eighty miles outside of San Antonio.

"This recipe's been in my family for over a hundred years" he brags, telling me about some mighty fine Texas barbecuing traditions. "You can smell this wonderful sop for miles, and it ain't bad on the meat either!" he adds. Felton guarantees that this recipe is great with beef or goat.

1 quart water

1 beef soup bone

1/8 cup Worcestershire sauce

1/8 cup white vinegar, or substitute the juice
  of 1 medium lemon

1 small onion, chopped

4 tablespoons cumin

2 tablespoons pepper

Combine the ingredients in a large stockpot. Cook mixture uncovered for 1 hour over low heat. Remove soup bone and simmer over medium heat 1/2 hour. Allow liquid to cool, then strain it. Use this sop over large cuts of meat. Then turn the meat over and sop it again.

Yield: 4 1/2 cups

From Felton Campbell of Campbell's Barbecue, Portland, Oregon

J. P. Hayes's Chipotle BBQ Sauce

Chef J. P. Hayes of Sgt. Pepper's Hot Sauce Microbrewery in Austin, Texas brews hot sauces, not beers. This is his favorite barbecue sauce because of the smoky flavor of the chipotle pepper.

2 whole ancho chiles, seeded

1 cup warm water

2 whole New Mexican chilies, seeded

1/2 can chipotles in adobo (available in most Hispanic markets)

1 cup water

1 teaspoon coarsely ground pepper

1 teaspoon cumin

1 teaspoon Mexican or regular oregano

1 teaspoon salt

1 tablespoon canola oil

1 medium onion, diced small

10 cloves garlic, roasted, peeled and chopped

1/2 cup cider vinegar

2 tablespoons balsamic vinegar

1/4 cup firmly packed brown sugar

1 1/2 cups ketchup

Rehydrate the ancho and New Mexican chiles in warm water until soft, about 15 minutes. Reserve soaking water. Purée the rehydrated chiles, chipotles in adobo, pepper, cumin, oregano, and salt, using enough of the chile soaking water to make a paste. Sauté the onion until translucent. Add roasted garlic and sauté for 5 minutes more. Add the chile purée, vinegars, brown sugar, and ketchup and simmer on low heat for 30 minutes.

Yield: 3 1/2 cups

From J. P. Hayes of Austin, Texas

The Best Ten Dollars Ever Written Off

The famous and staunchly guarded recipe for the sauce used by McClard's Barbecue of Hot Springs, Arkansas, came from a man who in 1928 couldn't pay his $10 room fee at Alex McClard's tourist court. Alex took the recipe in lieu of payment. Shortly thereafter, he opened up a barbecue stand and today McClard's is one of the country's most famous, oft-visited barbecue meccas.

Hollis's Cilantro & Lime Barbecue Sauce

Hollis loves to cook. He's been at it since he was a teenager, learning his craft in a variety of ethnic restaurants. Today, Hollis owns a very successful catering business which specializes in wood-smoked foods. You can sample Hollis's great food every fourth of July weekend at the Waterfront Blues Festival in Portland. Cilantro, by the way, is the Spanish name for coriander. This recipe is not only good for meat—it is also a great, fresh-tasting marinade for shellfish.

2 bunches cilantro, minced

5 cloves garlic, minced

1/2 cup Jamaican lime juice

1/2 cup olive oil

1 tablespoon dark soy sauce

1 tablespoon salt

Place all the ingredients into a food processor and purée until smooth. This sauce should be used immediately after you prepare it. For lamb, add a few sprigs of spearmint or peppermint.

Yield: 2 cups

From Hollis Harris of Porter's Catering Service, Portland, Oregon

Bruce's Spicy Raisin Sauce

This is an experiment which turned out lucky. It just goes to show you, experimentation can lead to some tasty results. This sauce is primarily used on pork—shoulders or butts or spareribs. Due to the high fructose content in the raisins, use this recipe as a finishing sauce or glaze.

4 cups seedless raisins

3 cups water

2 teaspoons cayenne

Put the raisins into a saucepan and add the water. Cook over medium heat until the raisins are plump and mushy. Strain the mixture. Reserve the liquid. Put the raisins in a food processor and blend. Strain the raisin pulp through a sieve, fine mesh flour strainer, or very dense cheesecloth. Add the reserved liquid. Add cayenne, more or less depending on the level of heat you want. Allow the mixture to cool before using as a glaze or finishing sauce.

To make into a thicker sauce, blend 1 tablespoon of cornstarch and 2 tablespoons of water, add it to the mixture, and simmer on low heat until thick.

Yield: 3 cups

From Bruce Bjorkman, Born 2 Que Team Krew, Oregon

Louisiana Jann's Sweet 'n' Tangy Sauce

Grand Chenier, located between Port Arthur and Pelican Island, Louisiana, is just about as far south as you can get in the central southern part of the United States. After Jann heard about this book from my editor at the Oregon Food Journal Magazine, *she was kind enough to send along an authentic Louisiana-style barbecue sauce.*

1 20-ounce bottle ketchup

3/4 cup firmly packed brown sugar

1/2 cup water

1/3 cup lemon juice

3 tablespoons dark mustard

2 tablespoons honey

2 tablespoons Worcestershire sauce

1/2 teaspoon vinegar

1 teaspoon garlic powder

1 package instant onion soup mix

1 small yellow onion, thinly sliced

1 small lemon, sliced into quarters
   and seeded

Combine all the ingredients except the lemon and onion in a medium sauce pan. Bring to a slow boil over medium heat. When liquid begins to boil, add onion and lemon slices. Cook sauce over medium heat for thirty minutes, until onion turns opaque. Remove the lemon quarters with a slotted spoon. Allow mixture to cool before using.

Yield: 4 cups

From Jann Jones of Grand Chenier, Louisiana

John Stage's Jalapeena Bar-B-Q Sauce

Dinosaur Barbecue jumps with the sound of the blues and the best barbecue to be found anywhere. You'll find a selection of sauces on the tables that complements the dry rub they use on their meat. This version has a little bite to it.

1/4 cup minced onion

1/2 green bell pepper, minced

3 Jalapeño peppers, seeded, minced

1/8 cup minced garlic

1/8 cup olive oil

1/2 cup beer

1/4 cup water

1/4 cup mustard

1/8 cup firmly packed brown sugar

1/8 cup Worcestershire sauce

1/4 cup Louisiana hot sauce

3/4 cup cider vinegar

1 teaspoon salt

1 teaspoon coarsely ground pepper

1 teaspoon chile powder

In a large saucepan, sauté onions, bell pepper, jalapeño, and garlic in oil until soft. Add beer and water, bring to a boil; reduce heat and add remaining ingredients. Slowly simmer, occasionally stirring, for about an hour.

Yield: 3 1/2 cups

From John Stage of Dinosaur Barbecue, Syracuse, New York

Hollis's Watermelon Barbecue Sauce

This is one of the most intriguing fruit-based sauces I've come across. Hollis has convinced me how good it is on chicken and fish like tuna, snapper, or kingfish.

1 6-pound seedless watermelon

8 ounces tomato paste

1 tablespoon onion powder

1 tablespoon garlic powder

2 cups firmly packed brown sugar

1/2 cup sherry

2 teaspoons lemon juice

1 teaspoon liquid smoke

Cut the melon into chunks and place in a saucepan. Cook it uncovered over medium heat until the melon is the consistency of applesauce (aproximately 2–3 hours). Stir it occasionally. Add remaining ingredients. Simmer uncovered over low heat for 2 hours. Allow to cool to room temperature before using.

Options: white vinegar may be substituted for the lemon juice. Try mixing yellow tomatoes and watermelon for color variation.

Yield: 2 cups

From Hollis Harris of Porter's Catering, Portland, Oregon

Bruce's Miss Peach, Mr. Bourbon Sauce

To my palate, nothing brings out the south like good bourbon and a tangy mustard-based sauce. Imagine how great life gets when you combine the two! This simple recipe is great as a coating for all cuts of pork. It does an excellent job in holding any rub mixture on the meat while cooking. As an added bonus, your pork will have a luscious golden color when it is done.

1 jar (8 ounces) Dijon mustard

1/4 cup peach jam

1/2 cup bourbon

In a saucepan, dissolve peach jam over low heat. Stir in mustard and bourbon until mixture is a smooth, medium consistency. This can be used a glaze if you are using indirect heat, or as a finishing sauce.

Yield: 2 cups

From Bruce Bjorkman, Born 2 Que Krew, of Salem, Oregon

A Whole Lot o' Cookin' Goin' On!

Joe Phelps, publisher of the *National Barbecue News,* estimates that on any given weekend in the United States, there may be twenty-three barbecue cookoff contests.

Rubs and Pastes

*R*ubs and pastes are an easy and excellent way to flavor any kind of meat or fish. The most important rule about rubs and pastes is balance. You want the rub to draw out the flavor of the meat, at the same time contributing to the overall taste experience.

Two essential ingredients are salt and sugar. Each of these acts as a carrier of the spices and aromatics, drawing them through the meat fibers as they dissolve while the meat is cooking. For many years, our Born 2 Que Krew cooking team shied away from using salt and sugar in the rubs we devised. In 1993 during the Annual Pacific Northwest Barbecue Association Pit Master course, we swallowed hard and used these two essential ingredients. You know what? The new rub with the salt and sugar tasted better after all.

If you are concerned about the amount of salt or sugar in your diet, cut back on the quantities used in these recipes. If you care about the sodium content in your food, be mindful of the amount of celery, onion, and garlic salts added to your rubs. You would be better off to use onion, garlic, and celery powders, which contain little or no salt.

This chapter includes rubs for specific meat and fish, like Sandi's Lamb Rub. Other rubs are universal—they go well with darn near anything. Rubs may be sprinkled on meats just prior to cooking, or allowed to soak into the meat while it is in the refrigerator overnight. Generally, the thicker the cut, the longer you want to let it sit with the rub on it before cooking.

Be precise in your measurements. Write down exactly what and how much of a particular seasoning you use. Experiment with the different herbs and spices. Once you've made up your rub recipe, store the mixture in an airtight container. Most rubs will hold their peak flavor for about three months.

Overleaf: the former Dixie Pit Bar-B-Q in Kansas City, Missouri; Don Elkins of The Central Texan Barbecue in Castroville, California

Bruce's BBQ Rub (circa 1993)

This is a rub I used to make without salt or sugar. However, the inclusion of sugar and salt helped make this a high-scoring, tasty rub in a barbecue competition one year. I find that it works well with beef, pork, and chicken.

1/2 cup firmly packed light brown sugar

1/2 cup white sugar

1/4 cup seasoned salt

1/4 onion powder

1/4 cup paprika

2 tablespoons pepper

2 tablespoons chile powder

2 tablespoons dry mustard

1 teaspoon poultry seasoning

1 teaspoon thyme

1 teaspoon tarragon

1 teaspoon ginger

1/2 teaspoon allspice

Place all ingredients in a resealable gallon-size freezer bag. Make sure bag is sealed. Shake and tumble the mixture until all ingredients are thoroughly mixed.

Yield: 2 cups

Note: I buy my herbs, such as thyme and tarragon, as whole leaves. Then I crush the leaves just before I make up the rub. Crush them as fine as possible—to a powder.

Sandi's Leg o' Lamb Rub

My wife Sandi has a discerning palate and I depend on her to help me put together rubs. Here's a recipe she concocted especially for lamb. I think it helps to turn a leg of lamb into an extremely tasty batch o' barbecue. This is enough rub for a 5 to 6-pound leg of lamb.

1/2 cup sugar

1/2 cup garlic salt

2 tablespoons garlic powder

2 tablespoons mint

1 teaspoon rosemary

Combine all ingredients into a sealable plastic freezer bag and seal the bag. Shake and toss the bag until the rub mixture is thoroughly mixed. Sprinkle over entire leg of lamb. Barbecue (indirect method) at 220°F for 8 to 10 hours, until an internal temperature of 165°F is reached in the thickest part of the leg.

Yield: 1 cup

Note: The mint and rosemary should be purchased as leaves, then pulverized just before you use them.

From Sandra Bjorkman, Born 2 Que Krew, Salem, Oregon

Rub for Beef & Pork

The following three rubs were developed especially for this volume by my barbecue friend Kim Wallis of St. Paul, Oregon. Kim got his first taste of real barbecue a few years ago, when on Super Bowl Sunday we stood outside in the damp Oregon snow, trying to barbecue a mess of ribs. Since that time Kim has developed into a very competent barbecuer in his own right.

1/2 cup firmly packed brown sugar

1/2 cup seasoned salt

1/2 cup paprika

2 tablespoons pepper

3 tablespoons chile powder

1 tablespoon onion granules

1 tablespoon garlic granules

1 tablespoon ginger

1/2 teaspoon cayenne

Mix ingredients together in an airtight container or freezer bag. Seal and shake thoroughly to mix.

Yield: 1 1/2 cups

From Kim Wallis of St. Paul, Oregon

Across the Road Rub

Poultry (chicken in particular) has become America's favorite meat for the grill. It must be a holdover from those Sunday chicken dinners we had at Grandma's when we were growing up.

6 tablespoons firmly packed brown sugar

3 tablespoons Spike seasoning

2 tablespoons paprika

1/2 teaspoon onion powder

1/4 teaspoon garlic powder

1/4 teaspoon pepper

1/4 teaspoon ginger

Place all ingredients in a resealable plastic bag, close, and shake to mix thoroughly.

Yield: 1 cup

Caution: Since this rub contains brown sugar, keep the chicken away from direct heat; otherwise the rub and the meat might scorch.

From Kim Wallis of St. Paul, Oregon

Mustard Seed Rub

This spicy, sweet, and not-too-hot rub tastes great on beef or chicken. The mustard seeds and marjoram add texture to the rub and help it form a delicious crust on the meat. Garam masala is a blend of sweet spices used frequently in East Indian cooking.

You can find garam masala in gourmet food stores or Indian markets; if not, you can make your own using the ingredients below. For best results, grind your spices fresh.

6 tablespoons garam masala (or the following blend)

  2 tablespoons freshly ground pepper

  2 tablespoons coriander

  1 tablespoon cardamom

  1/2 tablespoon cinnamon

  1/2 tablespoon cloves

1 1/2 cups firmly packed brown sugar

1/8 cup salt

1/8 cup paprika

1 tablespoon mustard seeds

1 tablespoon pasilla or ancho chiles (or ground chile powder)

1 teaspoon garlic granules

1 teaspoon ginger

1/2 teaspoon cumin

1/2 teaspoon marjoram

Place garam masala spices into a dry pan and roast over low heat until they begin to release their aroma. Let mixture cool. Grind to a coarse texture in a spice mill. Add to other ingredients in a sealable, airtight container or freezer bag, shake and toss ingredients until thoroughly mixed.

Yield: 2 1/2 cups

From Kim Wallis of St. Paul, Oregon

Tandoori Spice Rub

The tandoori is an oven used in East India for cooking. This rub will give chicken or fish the authentic flavor of food straight out of Bombay. It works well at high temperatures, so you can use it for either grilling or barbecuing.

1 teaspoon ginger

1 teaspoon cumin

1 teaspoon coriander

1 teaspoon paprika

1 teaspoon turmeric

1 teaspoon salt

1 teaspoon cayenne

Place all ingredients in a resealable plastic bag, close, and shake to mix thoroughly.

Yield: 2+ tablespoons

From Kim Wallis of St. Paul, Oregon

The Baron's No Salt Rub

You can count on one hand the number of individuals on the competition barbecue circuit who have won more ribbons than Paul Kirk, The Baron of Barbecue. A former executive chef for a Kansas City hospital, Paul is sympathetic to folks who maintain a salt-free diet, but still enjoy their food seasoned well. Here's one of Paul's own recipes for a tasty, salt-free rub that you can enjoy on any cut of meat.

1 cup sugar

3 1/2 tablespoons chile powder,
   New Mexico preferred

1 tablespoon sugar-free lemonade powder

1 tablespoon parsley flakes

1 tablespoon garlic powder

1 tablespoon onion powder

2 teaspoons celery seed

2 teaspoons freshly ground pepper

1 teaspoon basil

1 teaspoon marjoram

1 teaspoon sage

1 teaspoon cumin

1 teaspoon dry mustard

1 teaspoon dill weed

Combine ingredients in a bowl and mix thoroughly. Store unused rub in an airtight container.

Yield: 1 1/2 cups

From Paul Kirk, Ph.B., of Shawnee Mission, Kansas

Dennis Hayes's Basic Barbecue Rub

There's nothing fancy or earth-shattering about this rub—it's very simple. Use it on any type of meat, game, or fish with equally tasty results. This rub offers an excellent foundation from which to experiment and customize a rub of your own.

1/2 cup sugar

1/2 cup barbecue seasoning mix,
   or seasoned salt

1/4 cup salt

1 tablespoon dry mustard

1/2 teaspoon garlic powder

1/2 teaspoon paprika

1/2 teaspoon cayenne

Mix all ingredients thoroughly. Store in an airtight freezer bag or covered container.

Yield: 1 1/4 cups

From Dennis Hayes, late of Freedom, California, presently of Berkeley, California

 SAUCEMASTER TIP

If you're using tarragon in your recipes, try adding a dash of celery seed with it, and you'll enhance the flavor of this herb from France.

Jamaican Jerk Rub

Helen Willinsky's book Jerk: Barbecue from Jamaica *is responsible for getting me excited about the spicy Jamaican style of barbecuing, or jerk cooking. The term implies not only the way the meat is seasoned and cooked, but how it's prepared for the plate, jerked as opposed to cutting the meat. I think you'll enjoy her authentic recipe.*

1 medium onion

1/2 cup minced scallion

4 to 6 minced habanero peppers

2 teaspoons fresh thyme leaves

2 teaspoons salt

1 teaspoon allspice

1 teaspoon pepper

1/2 teaspoon cinnamon

1/4 teaspoon nutmeg

Put ingredients together in a food processor until they form a spreadable paste. Leftover rub may be stored in an airtight container for up to a month.

Yield: 1 cup

From Helen Willinsky, *Jerk: Barbecue from Jamaica,* The Crossing Press

Jamaican Jerk Rub #2

Jay Solomon, author of A Taste of the Tropics, *was introduced to island cooking a number of years ago when he visited the Caribbean. He came away from his adventure so enthusiastic that he opened his own tropical-theme restaurant. Jay's rub is not as hot as Helen's. It contains no habaneros.*

1 tablespoon allspice

1 tablespoon nutmeg

1 tablespoon cloves

1/2 tablespoon cinnamon

1/2 tablespoon mace

1 teaspoon thyme

1 teaspoon freshly ground pepper

Combine all ingredients in a resealable, air-tight freezer bag or container. Close tightly and shake until thoroughly mixed.

Yield: 1 cup

From Jay Solomon, *A Taste of the Tropics,* The Crossing Press

Jerk Rub #3

In Jamaica, there are as many recipes for jerk rubs as there are for barbecue sauces in the United States. All jerk rubs carry a few essential components, namely the fiery scotch bonnet pepper and Jamaican pimento, otherwise known as allspice.

1 onion, finely chopped

4 habaneros, seeded, deveined, and minced

1/2 cup minced scallions

2 teaspoons thyme

2 teaspoons salt

1 teaspoon allspice

1/4 teaspoon nutmeg

1/2 teaspoon cinnamon

1/2 teaspoon lemon peel

1 teaspoon pepper

Mix together all the ingredients to make a paste. A food processor fitted with a steel blade can help make this job go much faster and reduce the possibility of burning yourself. Be cautious when handling these peppers: they are capable of burning the skin, lips, and eyes! Store leftovers in the refrigerator in a tightly closed jar for about a month.

Yield: 1 cup

Rosemary Rub

Rosemary predominates in this rub. It's good on salmon steaks, chicken, or beef.

4 tablespoons chopped rosemary,
  or 3 tablespoons dried

2 teaspoons salt

1 tablespoon freshly cracked pepper

1/2 tablespoon freshly cracked white pepper

1/4 teaspoon cayenne

1 teaspoon dry mustard

1 teaspoon oregano

1 teaspoon garlic powder

Combine all ingredients in a spice mill or blender and grind to a coarse powder. Stored in an airtight jar, this will keep in the freezer for 3 to 4 months.

Yield: 1/2 cup

SAUCEMASTER TIP

To clean an electric coffee grinder that has been used to grind spices, throw in a small piece of bread and turn the grinder on for a few seconds. The bread will absorb any remaining loose spice. Shake out any bread crumbs left in the grinding chamber.

Big Easy Rub

Big flavor and ease of preparation are the essentials of this rub, which goes well with beef and pork. It has a good balance of sweetness, tang, and just a little heat from the white pepper.

1/2 cup firmly packed brown sugar

1/4 cup onion salt

1 tablespoon dry mustard

1 tablespoon paprika

1/2 tablespoon white pepper

Combine all ingredients in an airtight container or freezer bag. Shake thoroughly to mix.

Yield: 3/4 cup

Purely Pork Rub

This rub is best used with larger cuts of pork such as shoulders and the like, but it also goes well with tenderloin and spareribs.

2 tablespoons salt

2 tablespoons firmly packed brown sugar

2 tablespoons sugar

2 teaspoons paprika

2 teaspoons pepper

1 teaspoon cumin

1 teaspoon onion powder

1 teaspoon garlic powder

1/2 teaspoon cayenne

Combine ingredients in an airtight container or freezer bag. Shake and toss to mix.

Yield: 1/2 cup

Now we get to the best part of the whole damn deal. We sit down, tell some lies, and eat all this really good stuff!

—Sam Higgins, Texas barbecuer

Did you know?

- Pounds of charcoal briquets sold in 1994—804,127 tons

- Households in the United States—96,391,000

- Households who barbecue—71,329,340 (74%)

- Square footage of an average single family home—1,565 square feet

- Square footage of the ten barbecue grills used for the Arroyo Harbor, California Fourth of July fish cookout—2,100 square feet

- Percentage of barbecuers who clean their grills after every use—62%

- Amount of pork served in two days at the Memphis in May Barbecue Contest—38.5 tons

- Percentage annual increase in "upscale" barbecue sauce sales over the last three years—33%

- Number of charcoal-gas or pellet barbecues sold in 1994—12,384,981 representing 24 billion dollars in sales.

- Team that won the 1995 American Royal Invitational Barbecue Contest —Slaughterhouse Five; Westwood, KS

- Team that won the 1995 American Royal Open Barbecue Contest —Special Edition; Temple, TX

- Barbecue sauce that won the 1995 American Royal Sauce Contest —Paragon Firebrick BBQ Sauce; Claremore, OK

(Sources: Barbecue Industry Association; U.S. Statistical Abstract; May in Memphis; Mendocino Chamber of Commerce; National Association of Realtors; Houston Livestock Association; *1995 Information Please Almanac*)

Rub-a-Dub Barbecue Rub

The taste of cumin and cloves stands out in this rub. Try it on a pork roast.

1 cup paprika

1/4 cup cumin

1/4 cup firmly packed brown sugar

1/4 cup chile powder

1/4 cup salt

1/4 cup freshly cracked pepper

2 tablespoons cayenne

1 teaspoon cloves

Mix all the ingredients together. Stored covered in a cool, dark place, the rub will keep for about 6 weeks.

Yield: 2 cups

Country Spice Rub

The chile powder is unusual in this recipe . . . I've tried it on beef and pork ribs.

2 tablespoons chile powder

2 tablespoons cumin

2 tablespoons paprika

2 tablespoons pepper

2 tablespoons firmly packed brown sugar

2 teaspoons salt

1 teaspoon allspice

1 teaspoon cayenne

1/2 teaspoon cloves

Combine all ingredients and store in an airtight jar.

Yield: 1/3 cup

SAUCEMASTER TIP

Remus Powers says that there are three important considerations any saucemaster should remember.

1. Don't use too many ingredients.
2. Don't overuse liquid smoke.
3. Don't add too much celery seed to sauce or rubs.

Nice 'n' Naughty Rub

The tang of citrus peel is what makes this rub for pork and poultry one of the best. By increasing the cayenne, you make this rub naughty. By increasing the citrus and reducing the cayenne, you make it mostly nice. It depends on your mood.

1/4 cup salt

1/4 cup sugar

2 tablespoons lemon pepper

2 tablespoons allspice

1 tablespoon finely grated orange peel

1 tablespoon finely grated lemon peel

1 tablespoon finely grated lime peel

2 teaspoons cayenne

2 teaspoons mild paprika

Combine ingredients. Depending on how hot you care to make this rub, increase or reduce the amount of cayenne. Use teaspoon measurements when adding more cayenne to the recipe. Place unused mixture into an airtight freezer bag or container. It will store well in the refrigerator for three weeks.

Yield: 3/4 cup

Note: In lieu of grating the peels, you can run them through your food processor until very fine.

Sesame and Mustard Rub

The lime peel is unusual here. This recipe is good for shrimp, conch, and also, sausage links.

1 clove garlic, crushed

1 teaspoon mustard seeds

1/2 teaspoon finely slivered lime peel

2 teaspoons lime juice

2 tablespoons toasted sesame oil

Combine all ingredients in a bowl and mash until fairly smooth.

Yield: 3 1/2 tablespoons

SAUCEMASTER TIP

Paprika, the national spice of Hungary, is grown in six varieties, ranging in taste from mild to hot. Paprika is primarily used to add color to barbecue sauces. Spanish paprika is mostly used for this chore. The most flavorful paprika is Hungarian, characteristically warm in temperature with a more pungent flavor than the Spanish variety. Need to add more zip to your paprika? Add a dash of cayenne.

—Ann Wilder, Vann's Spices, Baltimore, Maryland

Li'l Devil Rub

This is great on a big chunk of beef.

1/4 cup grainy Dijon mustard

2 teaspoons olive oil

1/4 cup minced basil leaves

1/2 teaspoon freshly ground pepper

1/2 teaspoon chile powder

1/2 teaspoon cayenne, to taste

Dash of Tabasco, to taste (optional)

Combine all ingredients in a bowl. Mix thoroughly.

Yield: 1/2 cup

Hot 'n' Honey Rub

I love this on prime rib or prawns.

1/4 cup prepared horseradish

1 teaspoon chile powder

2 teaspoons soy sauce

2 teaspoons honey

Combine all ingredients in a bowl. Mash until smooth.

Yield: 1/3 cup

Garlic-Anchovy Rub

This is my favorite for chicken.

1 clove garlic, crushed

1 teaspoon anchovy paste

2 teaspoons olive oil

1/4 teaspoon freshly ground pepper

Combine all ingredients in a bowl. Mash until smooth.

Yield: 1 1/2 tablespoons

Leonard's Barbecue in Memphis, Tennessee (Elvis's favorite "Que" spot)

Cajun Rub

This is very flavorful on turkey and chicken.

2 tablespoons black peppercorns

2 tablespoons white peppercorns

1 to 2 tablespoons cayenne, to taste

3 tablespoons paprika

1 tablespoon firmly packed brown sugar

1 tablespoon salt, to taste

2 teaspoons garlic powder

2 teaspoons onion powder

2 teaspoons oregano

1 teaspoon sage

1 teaspoon thyme

Combine all ingredients in a blender or spice grinder and grind to a coarse powder.

Yield: 2/3 cup

Knife Knowledge

Ever wonder what those "dimples" are along the blade of a slicing knife? They allow a tiny pocket of air to form between the blade and the meat, letting the blade slice through the meat more evenly.

New Mexico Chile Rub

I've tried this on pork ribs and chicken.

3 tablespoons New Mexican chile powder

1 teaspoon Hungarian hot paprika

1/8 teaspoon coriander

2 to 3 tablespoons vegetable oil

Combine all ingredients in a bowl. Mash until smooth.

Yield: 1/3 cup

Latin-style Spice Rub

I know this is good on beef or pork roasts, maybe even sausage links. I'd try chorizo.

1/4 cup cumin

1/4 cup chile powder

2 tablespoons crushed coriander seeds

1 tablespoon cinnamon

1 tablespoon firmly packed brown sugar

2 tablespoons salt

1 tablespoon red pepper flakes

2 tablespoons freshly cracked pepper

Combine all the ingredients and grind to a powder in a spice mill, coffee grinder, or with a mortar and pestle. Covered in a cool, dark place, it will keep for about 6 weeks.

Yield: 1 cup

South Texas Rub

We've tried this on turkey parts or halves. Very good, either way.

2 cloves garlic, crushed
2 teaspoons seasoned pepper
2 teaspoons red pepper flakes
1/2 teaspoon cayenne, to taste
2 teaspoons seasoned salt

Combine all ingredients in a bowl. Mash until smooth.

Yield: 4 tablespoons

Basic Texas BBQ Dry Rub

I'd use this on any meat.

1 tablespoon salt
1 tablespoon pepper
1 tablespoon paprika
1 teaspoon dry mustard
1 tablespoon garlic granules
1 teaspoon celery seed
1 teaspoon chile powder

Combine all ingredients and store in an airtight plastic bag.

Yield: 5 tablespoons

The barbecue addict who is a seasoned traveler looks only at parking lots to prejudge a restaurant's product. If pickup trucks are parked next to expensive imports, he knows the barbecue is good.

—Gary D. Ford,
quoted in *Southern Living* magazine

Spicy San Antonio Rub

Heat this rub up or cool it down by varying the amount of cayenne you put into the mix. This is an especially good rub to use on beef brisket.

1/4 cup salt
1/4 cup pepper
2 tablespoons garlic powder
1 tablespoon cumin
1 tablespoon cayenne

Mix ingredients thoroughly in a plastic bowl or sealable freezer bag. Sprinkle on meat evenly on both sides; shake off excess rub.

Yield: 3/4 cup

Texas Tumbleweed Spice Mix

Chicken or turkey is your best bet here.

2 tablespoons paprika
1 tablespoon cayenne
1 teaspoon thyme
1 teaspoon oregano
1 teaspoon freshly ground black pepper
1 teaspoon freshly ground white pepper
1 tablespoon salt
1 tablespoon garlic powder
1 tablespoon onion powder

Combine all ingredients in an airtight jar. It will keep in the freezer for up to 6 months.

Yield: 1/2 cup

SAUCEMASTER TIP

Turmeric, a cousin to ginger, is widely grown in India. Many food companies use the spice as a secret ingredient in their prepared mustard barbecue sauces, and even in mayonnaise. Aside from its use as a spice, turmeric is used as a dye to color Buddhist monk's robes.

—Ann Wilder, Vann's Spices, Baltimore, Maryland

Sambal Mint Paste

I'd try a Satay (meat on a stick) with this recipe.

1/2 cup fresh mint leaves

1/2 cup fresh cilantro leaves

1/4 cup unsalted cashew pieces

1/2 cup tamarind juice

4 to 5 Thai bird peppers, or 3 to 4 dried red chile peppers, seeded

Combine all ingredients in a food processor and blend to a paste.

Yield: 1 cup

Traditional Tandoori

This is wonderful with chicken or a firm fish.

1 teaspoon ginger

1 teaspoon cumin

1 teaspoon coriander

1 teaspoon paprika

1 teaspoon turmeric

1 teaspoon salt

1 teaspoon cayenne

1/2 cup yogurt

2 tablespoons lemon juice

Combine all dry ingredients. Add the yogurt and lemon juice. Mix thoroughly. Coat the chicken or fish thoroughly. Allow the chicken or fish to marinate overnight in the refrigerator.

Yield: 1/3 cup

B.B.'s Lawnside Bar-B-Q in Kansas City, Missouri

Green Chile Paste

This is easy to assemble and very tasty too.

1 can (4 ounces) mild or hot green chiles
2 teaspoons chile powder
3 tablespoons vegetable oil

Combine all ingredients in a food processor. Process until smooth.

Yield: 1/3 cup

Molasses Paste

This is a handy little recipe to use when you are pinched for time. It can be used on poultry, beef, or pork.

2 1/2 tablespoons Dijon mustard
1/4 cup chili sauce
4 teaspoons molasses

Combine all ingredients in a bowl. Mix thoroughly.

Yield: 1/2 cup

Mixed Peppercorn Rub

The celery seeds and different peppercorns stand out in this recipe. Try it on almost anything. I'd start with chicken.

2 tablespoons black peppercorns
2 tablespoons white peppercorns
1 tablespoon pink peppercorns
1 tablespoon green peppercorns
1 tablespoon mustard seeds
1 tablespoon celery seeds
1 teaspoon garlic powder
1 teaspoon salt

Combine all ingredients in a spice grinder or blender and grind to a coarse meal.

Yield: 1/2 cup

SAUCEMASTER TIP

Too often overlooked, the herb savory, with its big, fragrant bouquet, tastes like a combination of oregano, thyme, sage, and pepper. It has a pleasant, bitter quality. Summer savory is slightly more delicate than winter savory, which smells like pine needles. Both savories are sharp in flavor. Of the two, summer savory is the more common; its flavor blends well with other herbs. It makes barbecued chicken especially succulent.

Yucatan Achiote Paste

You will find variations of this paste at the rotisserias in the Yucatan. The barbecue there is vibrant with the flavors of citrus and pepper.

1 1/2 cups water

1/2 cup annatto seeds,
  found in Latin markets

2 teaspoons olive oil

1 onion, coarsely chopped

4 cloves garlic, minced

2 serranos, seeded, membranes removed,
  finely minced

1/2 cup orange juice

1/4 cup grapefruit juice

1 teaspoon freshly cracked pepper

1/2 teaspoon salt, to taste

Juice of 1 lime, to taste

Place water in a saucepan over high heat. When the water boils, add the annatto seeds. Remove from heat and allow to soak 15 minutes. Drain and set aside the seeds. Discard the fluid.

Heat oil in a saucepan over medium heat. When hot, add onion and sauté 4 minutes, or until golden. Add garlic and serranos and cook 3 minutes. Add drained annatto seeds, fruit juices, and pepper. Season with salt. Bring to a boil. Lower heat and simmer about 10 minutes, or until remaining liquid in the pan is reduced to about 2 tablespoons. Add lime juice and remove from heat. Place in a blender and purée until smooth.

Yield: 4 cups

Roscoe's Rootbeer and Ribs in Rochester, Minnesota

Spicy Orange Paste

Chicken is your best bet here.s

1/4 cup orange juice

1/4 cup grapefruit juice

4 cloves garlic, chopped

1 habanero pepper, seeded and minced

2 tablespoons chopped cilantro

2 tablespoons annatto oil, or vegetable oil
with 1 teaspoon paprika

1 tablespoon lime juice

1 tablespoon red wine vinegar

2 teaspoons cumin

2 teaspoons oregano

1/2 teaspoon salt

1/2 teaspoon pepper

Combine all ingredients until they form a paste-like consistency.

Yield: 1 cup

SAUCEMASTER TIP

People complain to me that the outside of their meat chars and burns faster than the inside. This is usually the result of a fire being too hot and the meat being too thick. Most true barbecue restaurants either use a dry rub or cook the meat at low heat slowly over the pit until it is tender and then they add the sauce at the end of the cooking process, not while the meat is on the grill.

Dry rub can generally be used on any type of meat, not just chicken. Foods cooked with a dry rub turn out delicious, and the results can be enhanced still further by basting with a barbecue sauce during the final 5 minutes of cooking.

Resources

Mail Order Suppliers

Some of these companies may require minimum orders based on either a dollar amount or number of pounds ordered. One way to meet these minimums is to have a number of friends chip in with you to make the required purchase.

Spices

Ingredients Corporation of America, P.O. Box 240597, Memphis, TN 38124; (901) 454-0200. This company offers a full line of whole and ground spices, dehydrated herbs, botanicals, and essence oils. Custom blending available.

Milwaukee Seasonings, P.O. Box 339, Germantown, WI 53020; (800) 558-8696. You'll find a complete line of various seasoning blends, spices, and herbs.

Oregon Spice Company, 1630 SE Rhine, Portland, OR 97202; (503) 238-0664. This company carries a full line of domestic and imported spices in institutional sizes. Custom blending available.

G. B. Ratto & Company, 821 Washington Street, Oakland, CA 94607; (800) 325-3483. One of the oldest spice suppliers on the West Coast.

Razorback Barbecue Seasonings, P.O. Box 631, Blytheville, AR 72316; (501) 763-6392. Authentic Arkansas seasonings and spice mixtures from a barbecue legend, Ray Gill.

Spiceland, Inc., 3206 North Major, Chicago, IL 60634; (312) 736-1000.

Texas Spice Company, 1826 Enchanted Lane, Lancaster, TX 75146-3521; (214) 227-0686. Home of the famous "Yankee Blaster" spice mixture, Texas Spice is a distributor of many different spices and rubs.

Vann's Spices Ltd., 1238 Joppa Road, Baltimore, MD 21286; (410) 583-1643. Vann's carries a complete product line of imported and domestic herbs, spices and custom seasonings, including some unique items like granulated honey. Custom blending available.

Overleaf: A & R Bar-B-Q in Memphis, Tennessee

*M*y two favorite spices? Ginger and rosemary. I call 'em my girlfriends.

—Paul Kirk,
The Kansas City Baron of Barbecue

Sauces

Here is a list of some of the country's most flavorful, famous, and unique barbecue sauces. This is by no means a complete list, because half the fun of barbecue is discovering your own "motherlode."

Arthur Bryant's A Kansas City legend, this is a sauce that will have you gnawing off your fingertips to get every succulent drop. (816) 231-1123

Billy Bones Sanford, Michigan, is home to this infamous "rib burner." Billy told me he spent 16 years developing this sauce. It's a tomato-based wonder with a kick. (517) 687-7880

Charcoal Companion, the best source for top quality barbecue tools and accessories also makes a number of excellent sauces and spice rubs. (800) 521-0505

Corky's This venerable favorite in Memphis is fast becoming a modern-day barbecue legend. Corky's will be happy to send you next-day delivery some of their tasty "que." (800) 926-7597

Dragon's Breath A regional classic mustard-based sauce. You definitely want to add this favorite to your kitchen. (800) 215-5422

Dreamland Barbecue "Yes sir, it's cooked in de pit" is the motto emblazoned on their menus, t-shirts, and barbecue sauce. This is a sauce from Alabama. (800) 752-0544

Maurice's Carolina Gold If ever anyone could be proclaimed the Walt Disney of barbecue, it's Maurice Bessinger's Piggy Park in West Columbia, South Carolina. Here's an authentic tangy mustard-based sauce from one of the originators of airborne barbecue! (800) 628-7423

McClard's This is the "million dollar" sauce that was handed over in lieu of paying for a night's lodging. McClard's sauce is hot, thin, and sweet, and it costs less than a million to try some. (501) 767-4063

Ollie's Barbecue This sauce is most unusual in that Ollie puts celery seed in it. (205) 324-9485

Roscoe's Barbecue Sauce Leave it to an enterprising Steve "Roscoe" Ross to take an old A&W drive-in and turn the place into a smokin' success. He makes a great sauce, too. (800) 369-7427

Sonny's This is the quintessential Texas classic well worth making a special trip to the "Big D" for a taste. (800) 576-6697

Stonewall Chili Pepper Company Not for the faint of tongue. (800) 232-2995

The Great Southern Sauce Company Can't decide which sauce to try? These folks make it easy with a full assortment of the South's most famous sauces. (800) 437-2823

Mustard

To my tastebuds, there's nothing that complements barbecued pork like a good spicy mustard. You'll be glad to learn there's one source for more than 2,500 different types of mustard: the Mount Horeb Mustard Museum. To receive a price list and catalog dial (800) 438-6878

Associations

These nonprofit organizations are dedicated to fanning the flame of our favorite pastime.

International Barbecue Cookers Association (IBCA), P.O. Box 300566, Arlington, TX 76007-0556; (817) 469-1579. This organization sanctions barbecue cook-offs throughout Texas and the Southwest. Dues: $25/year. Monthly newspaper subscriptions extra.

Kansas City Barbecue Society (KCBS), 11514 Hickman Mills Drive, Kansas City, MO 64134; (800) 963-KCBS. Boasting more than 1,000 members around the world, KCBS sanctions contests and promotes the annual American Royal Championship Barbecue Cookoff. They also publish The Bull Sheet, a monthly cornucopia of barbecue information.

Memphis In May, 245 Wagner Place, Suite 220, Memphis, TN 38103; (901) 525-4611. This organization sanctions pork-only barbecue cookoffs throughout the South, and coordinates the prestigious Memphis In May World Championship Barbecue Cookoff every year.

National Barbecue Association (NBBQA), 723 S. Sharon Amity Road, Suite 214, Charlotte, NC 28211; (704) 365-3622. The NBBQA is dedicated to promoting all aspects of barbecuing, both on a professional and amateur basis. The association publishes a monthly newsletter, *Barbecue Today*; hosts an annual convention and trade show; and is a great resource for barbecue lovers. Dues: $35 non-business members; $75 business members.

Pacific Northwest Barbecue Association, 4244 134th Avenue S.E., Bellevue, WA 98006; (206) 643-0607. The PNWBA promotes an annual barbecue contest circuit, sponsors training sessions, and publishes a quarterly newsletter, *Drippings from the Pit*. Dues are just $10 a year.

The Dakota Kid Team of West Linn, Oregon

Other Sources of Barbecue Information

Chile Pepper Magazine, P.O. Box 769, Mt. Morris, IL 61054-0769; (800) 959-5468. While the focus of this glossy monthly magazine is primarily chiles, they feature a brisk-selling annual issue about barbecue, and from time to time publish articles about various barbecue restaurants around the country. Dave DeWitt, editor of the magazine, is also a Crossing Press author. $18.95/year.

The Crossing Press, P.O. Box 1048, Freedom, CA 95019; (800) 777-1048. Write or call for their free cookbook catalog offering many good books with hot and spicy recipes. Check out their *Marinades* and *The Hot Sauce Bible*.

The National Barbecue News, P.O. Box 923, Douglas, GA 31533; (800) 384-0002. This is the "original" monthly barbecue newspaper, featuring contest information, columns (including the author's), and valuable barbecue resource information. $18/year.

The Pits, 7714 Hillard, Dallas, TX 75217. Monthly paper. $18/year.

Cooking Up Barbecue in a Big Way

Don Gillis, editor of the *National Barbecue News,* Douglas, Georgia, lists the five largest barbecue competitions in the country, based on the number of teams participating:

1. American Royal/Diddy-Wa-Diddy Sauce Contest; Kansas City, Missouri; October
2. Memphis-In-May World Championship Barbecue Cookoff; Memphis, Tennessee; May
3. Houston Livestock Show/Barbecue Cook-off; Houston, Texas; January
4. Big Pig Jig; Vienna, Georgia; October
5. Taylor Texas Invitational; Taylor, Texas; August

Bibliography

Barbecue books are a lot like eating potato chips, you just can't stop at one. The following are some notable books on barbecue and cooking worthy of your pantry shelf or library.

1995 Davis, Rich, & Stein, Shifra. *All About Barbecue Kansas City Style.* Kansas City: Pig Out Publications.

1988 Davis, Rich, & Stein, Shifra. *All American Barbecue Book.* New York: Vintage Originals.

1993 Dominguez, Jan Roberts. *The Mustard Book.* New York: Macmillan.

1994 Egerton, John. *Southern Food: At Home, On the Road, In History.* Chapel Hill: University of North Carolina Press.

1992 Kansas City Barbecue Society. *The Passion of Barbecue.* New York: Hyperion.

1994 Permenter, Paris, & Bigley, John. *Texas Barbecue.* Kansas City: Pig Out Publications.

1974 Rombauer, Irma S., & Becker, Marion R. *The Joy of Cooking,* Indianapolis: Bobbs-Merrill Company.

1995 Smith, Andrew F. *The Tomato in America,* Columbia: University of South Carolina Press.

1994 Tarantino, James. *Marinades.* Freedom: The Crossing Press.

1979 Wall, Patricia, & Layne, Ron. *Hog Heaven.* Lexington, South Carolina: The Sandpiper Store.

1990 Willinsky, Helen. *Jerk Barbecue from Jamaica.* Freedom: The Crossing Press.

Calendar of Barbecue Competitions

sanctioned by the Kansas City Barbecue Society

April

Galena Spring Fling. Galena, KS. Contact: Larry Oglesby, c.o. United Automotive, Galena, KS 66739 or call 316/783-2459.

Southeast Regional Championship Barbecue Contest. Contact: Herb Cathey, 719 47th St. W., Palmetto, FL 34221 or call 813/722-9622.

Annual Oklahoma Lan Run Barbecue Cookoff, Oklahoma City, OK. To benefit hospice of Oklahoma County. Contact: Dale Hamilton, 700 NE 13th St., Oklahoma City, OK 73104 or 405/271-6601.

Annual KCBS Spring Training, Bucyrus, KS. For more information contact: KCBS, 11514 Hickman Mills Dr., KC MO 64134 or call 316/765-5891.

Annual Olde Town Barbecue Cookoff. Contact: Jim Siebert, 5330 E. Crestview, Wichita, KS 67208 or 316/684-0478.

May

Annual Blue Devil Barbecue Cookoff, KC, KS. Contact: Karen L. Atchley/KCKCC Endowment Assoc., 7250 State Ave., KC, KS 66112 or 913/596-9632 or 913/334-1100 ext. 632 or Fax 913/596-9663.

Annual Raytown Barbecue Cookoff, Raytown, MO. Contact: Quentin Clark, 9715 E. 63Rd St., Raytown, MO 64133 or 816/356-0505.

KWQC-TV 6 Annual Barbecue Cookoff, Davenport, IA. Held across the river in Rock Island, IL. Sponsored by Jumer's Casino Rock Island. Contact Wil Rogers, 805 Brady St., Davenport,, IA 52808 or 319/383-7000.

Annual Oklahoma Joe's Interplanetary BBQ Championship, Perry, OK. Contact: Joe Davidson, PO Box 835, Perry, OK 73077 or call 405/336-3080.

June

Annual McLouth Prairie Days BBQ Blow Out, McLouth, KS. Contact: Marlin McAferty, PO Box 116, McLouth, KS 66054 or 913/796-6112 (d) or 913/796-6737 (e).

Annual NKC Missouri State Championship BBQ. Contact: Hobart Mason, 203 E. 11th, N. Kansas City, MO 64116 or 816/471-4895.

Blue Ridge Barbecue and Musical Festival, Tryon, NC. North Carolina State Championship. Contact: Chamber of Commerce, 401 N. Trade St., Tryon, NC 28782 or 704/859-6236.

Stockyards Stampede Barbecue Cookoff, Edmond, OK. Contact: Chris Rude, PO Box 5255, Edmond, OK 73083-5255 or 405/348-1233.

Annual Grain Valley BBQ Contest, Grain Valley, MO. Contact: Sharon Stewart, PO Box 447, Grain Valley, MO 64029 or 816/229-2875 or CJ 816/224-8808.

The Great Show-Me-State Barbecue Championship, St. Joseph, MO. Held at the Civic Center Park. Contact: Steve Culver, Rt 1, Box 225, Easton, MO 6443 or 816/677-5520.

Annual Greater Slater BBQ Open, Slater, MO. Contact: Bud Summers, PO Box 100, Slater, MO 65349 or 816/529-2222 (d) or 816/784-2538 or Fax: 816/529-2660.

Sunday BarbeQlossal, Indianapolis, IN at the Indiana State Fairgrounds part of World Pork Expo. Contact: Ernie Barnes, Ann Rehnstrom, Becky Pattschull, PO Box 10383, Des Moines, IA 50306 or 515/223-2751.

Annual Lexington BBQ Bail-Out, Lexington, MO. Contact: Bill Rousseau, PO Box 714, Grain Valley, MO 64029 or 816/229-2225.

Annual Fox Valley BBQ Championship, Oswego, IL. Contact: William (Bill) Penn, 4500 Rt 71, Oswego, IL 60543 or 708/554-3389.

Chief Osceola BBQ Pow Wow (Raft Canoe Race). This is a contest to sell your food to the public besides competing. For more info: Cecil Pritchett, PO Box J, Osceola, MO 64776 or 417/646-8829 or 1-800-423-2451.

July

Annual Illinois State BBQ Championship, West Chicago, IL. Contact: Jim Burns, 1200 W. Hawthorne, West Chicago, IL 60185 or 708/231-6262 or Fax: 708/231-6280.

Annual Cherokee Strip BBQ Cookoff. Contact: Debbie Whitener, 3624 Wellington Rd., Ponca City, OK 74604 or 405/767-1698.

Annual Midwest Regional Barbecue Championship, Gladstone, MO. Contact: Nelsie Sweeney/Gladstone Area Chamber of Commerce, PO Box 10751, Gladstone, MO 64118 or call 816/436-4528.

Annual Kay County BBQ & Chili Cookoff, Kay County Fairgrounds, Blackwell, OK. Contact: DeWayne Muret, PO Box 434, Tonkawa, OK 74653 or 405/628-3228 (d) or 405/363-3394 (e).

Piper Prairie Days BBQ Contest, Piper, KS. Location at the Agricultural Hall of Fame in Bonner Springs, KS. Contact: Craig Howell, 12117 Leavenworth Rd., KC, KS 66109 or 913/721-1163.

Dodge City Days Barbecue Contest, Dodge City, KS. Contact: Pat Shrader, Dodge City Area Chamber of Commerce, 4th & Spruce, Dodge City, KS 67801 or 316/227-3119.

August

Annual Village of Laurie, Laurie, MO. Contact: Shirley Jobe, PO Box 1054, Laurie, MO 65308 or 314/372-0558 (M–F 9:00 am–4:00 pm call 315/374-4871).

Sizzlin' Summer Cookoff, Joplin, MO. Contact: Sherry Shultz, 2905 E. 4th Street, Joplin, MO 64801 or 417/623-2107. Fax: 782-5111.

The Woodlands/Adrians BBQ Cookoff. For more info: Jill Gromer, 913/299-9797.

Jo Co Fair BBQ Contest, Johnson County, Stilwell, KS. Contact: Dave Webb, 18001 Nall, Stilwell, KS 66088 or 913/681-8600.

Ribs N Racin' II, Lakeside Speedway, KC, KS. Contact: Dan Smith, 5615 Wolcott Dr., KC, KS 66109 or 816/374-5874 or 913/299-2040.

Annual D.C. Barbecue Championship held by the National Kidney Foundation, Washington, D.C. Sponsored by DC101 and Red Hot & Blue. All proceeds will benefit programs in research, professional and public education, and patient and community services in the area. For more information contact: Kevin Heffner, 5335 Wisconsin Ave., N.W., Suite 830, Washington, D.C. 20015-2030 or 202/244-7900.

City of Cookeville, TN. Contact: Ricky Shelton, 560 S. Jefferson Ave., Cookeville, TN 38501 or 615/526-2354.

September

Elk Lodge Blazethon, Stillwater, OK. For more info: Stillwater Elks Lodge #1859, 202 McElroy, Stillwater, OK 74075 or 405/733-3300.

Blue Springs Missouri State Championship Barbeque Contest, Blue Springs, MO. Contact: Kent Edmondson, 1709 Ash Street, Blue Springs, MO 64015, 816/229-4864 or Pam Buck, 903 Main Street, Blue Springs, MO 64015 or 816/228-0137.

Step West KFDI Barbecue Fest, Wichita, KS. Contact: Kathleen Wille, PO Box 1402, Wichita, KS 67201 or 316/838-9141.

Blue Grass & Chili & BBQ Festival, Tulsa, OK. Contact: Dell Davis, 918/583-2617 or 201 W. 5th, Suite 450, Tulsa, OK 74103.

Annual Jesse James Barbeque Cook Out (part of Missouri State Championship). Contact: Larry Pratt, PO Box 202, Kearney, MO 64060 or 816/635-4502 or 816/274-8580.

Bates County Barbecue Championship, Butler, MO. Contact: Al Decker, PO Box 12, Butler, MO 64730 or call 816/679-3380.

North Carolina BBQ Championship held in City park in conjunction with the Burlington, NC Carousel Festival. Contact: Jim Mason, 1-800-222-7566 ext. 3538.

Ottawa Prairie Fire Cookoff. Contact: Diane Korte, 913/294-4311.

Annual State BBQ Championships of Nebraska. As part of River City Roundup. Greater Omaha Barbecue Society. Contact: Byron Bissel, 5724 N. 97th St., Omaha, NE 68134 or Joan Matoole, 402/393-4376.

October

American Royal Barbecue Contest. Largest Barbecue Contest in the World. Kansas City, MO. Contact: Pam McKee, 1701 American Royal Court, KC, MO 64108 or 816/221-9800.

Byhalia, MS Barbeque Cooking Contest. Contact: Tommy Woods, 601/838-6754.

Annual Pig & Pepper Harvest, Westford, MA. Contact: Bob Rothenberg, Carlisle Education Foundation, 91 Carleton Rd., Carlisle, MA 01741 or 508/369-0366. Pig & Pepper Info Line.

Jack Daniels World Championship Invitational, Lynchburg, TN. An invitation contest only for Grand Champions. Contact: Peggy Vessels, 615/327-1551.

November

Annual Florida State Championship Barbeque Contest. Contact: Herb Cathey, 719 47th St., W., Palmetto, FL 34221 or 813/722-9622.

For a current catalog of books from
The Crossing Press, please visit our
Web site: **www.tenspeed.com**.